EVANGELISM AND MISSIONS

EVANGELISM AND MISSIONS

D. SCOTT HILDRETH

Printed in the United States of America

978-1-4300-9657-3

Published by B&H Publishing Group
Brentwood, Tennessee

Dewey Decimal Classification: 269.2
Subject Heading: EVANGELISTIC WORK
/ MISSIONS / WITNESSING

Cover design by Matt Lehman.

1 2 3 4 5 6 • 28 27 26 25

This book is for Lesley.
I told you we'd see the world together.

Acknowledgments

The lessons and content of this book are only possible because of those who have walked with me through the years as I have sought to explore the depth and breadth of God's grand mission.

From Christians around the world I have gained a deeper insight into the joy and cost of faith in Jesus.

For my students at Southeastern Seminary and Judson College: your patience, probing questions, and enthusiasm from the classroom has made me a better thinker and missiologist.

To fellow missionaries along the way. I will always be honored to have been one of your number.

To Danny Akin and my colleagues at SEBTS: I will never be able to thank you enough for your partnership in the gospel.

To my Summit family, elders, and small group, it is always challenging to learn with you what it means to live out the commission: "You are Sent."

Contents

Introduction 1

Chapter 1: Am I Really Responsible for the Whole World? 17

Chapter 2: By What Authority Do We Go? 43

Chapter 3: Who in the World Are We Trying to Reach? 61

Chapter 4: What about Other Gods? 81

Chapter 5: What Is the Missionary Task? 105

Conclusion 133

About the Author 135

Notes 137

Introduction

IN 1792, WILLIAM CAREY stood before a room of Baptist pastors and preached one of the most famous mission sermons ever: "An Enquiry into the Obligation of Christians to Use Means for the Conversion of the Heathen." The sermon was an impassioned plea for British Baptist pastors to rally their churches for the cause of global missions. Most historians point to this sermon as the beginning of the modern missionary movement.

The backstory begins with Carey reading the travel journals of Captain James Cook, the famous British explorer. His stories and descriptions of faraway places stirred Carey's imagination. While most readers must have been swept up in the tales of adventure in exotic places, Carey's heart was consumed by the vast lostness of the world. The more he learned, the more convinced he became that God's will for all Christians included the responsibility of seeking the salvation of those who had never heard the gospel and, as a result, lived in spiritual darkness.

Carey's sermon text that day was the Great Commission found at the end of the Gospel of Matthew: "All authority has been given to me in heaven and on earth. Go, therefore, and make disciples of all nations, baptizing them in the name of the Father and of the Son and of the Holy Spirit, teaching them to observe everything I have commanded you. And remember, I am with you always, to the end of the age" (Matt. 28:18–20).

With reference to this text, he preached:

> This commission was as extensive as possible, and laid them under obligation to disperse themselves into every country to the habitable globe, and preach to all inhabitants, without exception or limitation. . . . But the work has not been taken up, or prosecuted of late years (except by a few individuals). . . . It is thus that multitudes sit at ease, and give themselves no concern about the far greater parts of their fellow sinners, who to this day, are lost in ignorance and idolatry.[1]

At the end of this sermon, one of the more senior and respected pastors in the area, John Ryland Sr., stood and rebuked Carey for being presumptuous. "Young man, sit down." His voice thundered in the room. "When God pleases to convert the heathen, he will do it without your aid or mine."

What was Carey's error? Why did this missionary sermon elicit such a strong reaction? The answer lies in his inclusion of one simple phrase in the sermon title, "*to use means.*" You see, in Carey's day, a prevailing theological belief was that God's sovereign control of the universe meant he had predestined some souls for heaven and others for hell. It was a waste of time (if not an outright insult to God's plan) for Christians to make extraordinary efforts to win others to Christ. If it were God's will for them to be saved, he would do it on his own.

Carey's sermon challenged this belief. In fact, his message pushed forward the conviction that Jesus's command at the end of Matthew created an obligation for Christians to do something, to be intentional, focused, and creative in seeking to win those to Jesus who had never heard. As he drew his message to a close, Carey said:

> We must not be contented, however with praying, without exerting ourselves in the use

> of means for the obtaining of those things we pray for. Were the children of the light as wise as children of this world they would stretch every nerve to gain so glorious a prize, nor ever imagine that it was to be obtained in any other way. . . .
>
> What a heaven it will be to see the many myriads of poor heathens, of Britons, amongst the rest, who by their labors have been brought to the knowledge of God. Surely a crown of rejoicing like this is worth aspiring to. Surely it is worthwhile to lay ourselves with all our might in promoting the cause and the kingdom of Christ.[2]

Despite John Ryland's objection, Carey's *Enquiry* sermon generated such movement among British Baptists that the entire story of evangelical/Protestant missions is written from this point forward. Carey is known as the Father of Modern Missions because of his influence in helping develop the Baptist Mission Society and then serving as a missionary in India. Because of his leadership, the missionary team translated the Bible into several South Asian languages, established schools and pastor training facilities, and even played a significant role in overturning the custom of widow burning.

I have no delusions of being another Carey; however, this book is my attempt to strike a similar note of encouragement and inspiration. Christians in the West too often seem content to allow the rest of the world to live a Christless existence and die, facing a Christless eternity. We prioritize politics, economics, personal comfort, and even petty theological squabbles to distract us from the Great Commission. Whether those in need of Christ include our neighbor across the street, our coworker down the hall, or the unreached people group on the other side of the world, far too many of us live out the words of John Ryland: "If God wants to reach them, he can do it without my help."[3] While most of us would never utter these words aloud, too often our lives reflect the sentiment.

MISSIONS AND EVANGELISM

In the middle of the twentieth century, the global church faced a crisis of mission. Countries that had previously served as missionary-sending nations had spent the better part of the previous two decades destroying the world through a series of wars. To make matters worse, in many instances, pulpits served as mouthpieces of war efforts on both sides of the conflicts. In the shadow of this backdrop, the pressing question before Christian leaders was: What is missions? If one defined it as any ministry the church undertakes in the name of God, then the previous decades created a serious confusion.

One corrective idea emerged from these discussions: following the writings of several theologians, church leaders embraced the idea of "mission of God." (The common Latin phrase for this phrase is *missio Dei.*) This theological concept advanced the idea that missions should not be reduced to the activities of the local church. Rather, mission is a movement rooted in the character of God himself. It is his mission, and he has called his people to join him in fulfilling his goals and agenda. Missiologist David Bosch notes, "In the new image mission is not primarily an activity of the church, but an attribute of God. . . . Mission is thereby seen as a movement from God to the world; the church is viewed as an instrument for that Mission."[4]

This idea of the *mission of God* provided helpful correction in the aftermath of the world wars; however, it also introduced some confusion into the conversation. When missiologists advanced a new understanding of the origin of missions and it was disconnected from the church's work, some began to advocate a more secular or social understanding of *mission*. As Bosch observed, with the unhitching of mission from the activity of the church, many took the teaching to mean that mission "excluded the church's involvement"[5] altogether. Lesslie Newbigin described this situation with stunning clarity:

> If God is indeed the true missionary, it was said, our business is not to promote the mission of the church, but to get out into the world, find out "what God is doing in the world," and join forces with him. And "what God is doing" was generally thought to be in the secular rather than in the religious sectors of human life. The effect of course, was to look for what seemed to be the rising powers and to identify Christian missionary responsibility with support for a range of political and cultural developments.[6]

This divergence in the understanding of missions eventually caused a split in the global Protestant church. One stream (the "mainline") advocated the understanding of mission as a movement that takes place primarily outside the church, measured more by social, political, and/or economic agendas. The newer stream (which eventually became known as *evangelicals*) rejected this broad understanding in favor of keeping missions rooted in the evangelistic work of the gospel. While never rejecting the significance of social activity and benevolent care, evangelicals maintained an understanding of missions that emphasized the proclamation of the Christian gospel with the anticipation of personal conversion, spiritual sanctification, and church growth. This book is not only built on this evangelical understanding of missions, but it also serves as a call for evangelicals to embrace our origins, being reminded that Jesus best summarizes God's mission when he said: "For the Son of Man has come to seek and to save the lost" (Luke 19:10).

With this strong emphasis on evangelism and proclamation, some rightfully ask about the relationship between evangelical activities and social engagement. Should we simply preach the gospel and leave the more immediate needs to governments, aid agencies, or special interest groups? Of course not; this would be an insult to the nature of humanity and the basic command of Jesus to love our neighbors.

Over the years, I have found it helpful to illustrate this relationship by pointing to a bicycle. More specifically, to the contrasting functions of the bicycle wheels when we imagine the front wheel representing compassion or holistic ministries and the back wheel representing proclamation ministries. While it is possible to move on just the front wheel, eventually the bicycle will lose momentum and fall. At the same time, it is possible to bicycle using the back wheel alone, and with a strong pedal and careful balance, one might even travel further. But this is not the design of the bicycle. If we only use the back wheel, the bike will be out of balance and will struggle to stay on course. Both wheels are necessary for the bicycle to function properly. The front wheel (the holistic ministries) provides direction and support while the back wheel (the proclamation ministry) supplies the power and energy to keep everything moving. When asked to prioritize effort, the rider will always focus on the back wheel. But, if she neglects the front wheel, things quickly veer off course.

The goal of this book is to provide motivation as well as practical tools for you to embrace God's mission as your framework for life. First, we will meditate on the different themes found in the Great Commission (Matt. 28:18–20). This journey will help you understand God's heart and vision for the world and for your life. Alongside this biblical study, we will take time to learn about the world and the desperate needs of those who live in spiritual darkness. We will learn about different religions as well as learn to see the globe through God's eyes. Along the way, we will learn some practical guidelines that will help you be more involved in God's work of saving the lost and redeeming a fallen world through Jesus.

WHY A NEW BOOK ON MISSIONS AND EVANGELISM?

This is a fair question. In fact, the writer of Ecclesiastes once wrote, "Be warned: there is no end to the making of many books" (Eccles. 12:12). So, with this biblical warning in mind, why write a new book about missions? The plain answer is that the world is changing around us, and these changes bring with them a need to call the church back to our central task of making disciples in our neighborhoods and places where we live our regular lives, as well as taking the gospel to the ends of the earth.

The global upheaval that resulted from the COVID pandemic and social unrest has made the world a more dangerous place, but it has also exposed the desperate need for the Christian gospel. Many governments use health and safety to justify intense monitoring of their citizens. This use of technology has also exposed many Christians to deeper levels of persecution. Travel restrictions and global "finger pointing" have exaggerated the situation, even serving as justification for national prejudices and xenophobia. These changes make missionary work much more complicated.

In the United States, the Christian message has been tagged as hateful by many in the public square. We read stories (or watch YouTube testimonies) of so-called *Christian influencers* deconstructing their faith and walking away from the gospel. Evangelism is viewed as arrogant, if not unethical, by some. This pressure tempts many well-intentioned Christians to opt for silence rather than winsome sharing of their faith. The U.S. is a top migration destination. This means we are surrounded by people who need Jesus, many arriving in this free country from countries with significant religious restrictions. However, some American Christians have reduced the migration phenomenon to a political issue rather than see it as a missions opportunity.

At the same time, as in every generation, Christians face the temptation to apply our faith as a social or political movement. The name *evangelical* loses its force when the movement becomes a voting block rather than a people who proclaim the life-changing message of Jesus. Like Esau, some are guilty of selling our birthright for momentary pressures. Rather than holding to the path that has been charted by our predecessors—keeping the proclamation of the message of salvation through Jesus as our missionary goal—some embrace a vision of God's mission as a social, political, or cultural movement. While these decisions may differ from the more radical teachings of the Protestant liberals of the 1950s, the central emphasis is the same. The fulfillment of God's mission has been relocated outside the church. I hope this book will serve as a challenge for Christians today to embrace this moment as our time to "shine like stars in the world" (Phil. 2:15).

As I think about our present moment, I'm reminded of the conversation between Frodo Baggins and Gandalf in *The Lord of the Rings.* After listening to Gandalf explain the desperation of the moment, Frodo replies: "I wish it need not have happened in my time."

Gandalf answers, "So do I. . . . And so do all who live to see such times. But that is not for them to decide. All we have to decide is what to do with the time that is given to us."[7]

We face difficult days indeed. We don't need to wonder if this is the most complicated moment in history. I am sure for some it is, and for others it isn't. However, we can be sure it is our moment. The Lord of history has called us to his mission at this time. We dare not shrink back or let fear drive us into silence.

The rest of this book will be a meditation on Jesus's final words to his disciples in the book of Matthew, the Great Commission: "All authority has been given to me in heaven and on earth. Go, therefore, and make disciples of all nations, baptizing them in the name of the Father and of the Son and of the Holy Spirit, teaching them to observe everything I have commanded you. And remember, I am with you always, to the end of the age" (Matt. 28:18–20).

We will answer questions about our personal callings and our responsibility for the nations and our neighbors. We will also consider what it means for us to live on mission in submission to Jesus as our ever-present King. Along the way, this book will help you understand the world around you as we explore world religions and other barriers against faith. The book also includes points of practical application designed to provide clear handles for you to live a life of evangelism and missions.

Thanks for reading. I pray that the Lord uses this book to awaken the missionary within you. And, as a result, many will hear the gospel and respond, moving from darkness to light as they embrace the life-changing message: "For God loved the world in this way: He gave his one and only Son, so that everyone who believes in him will not perish but have eternal life. For God did not send his Son into the world to condemn the world, but to save the world through him" (John 3:16–17).

DISCUSS AND REFLECT

1. What are you most excited to learn as you think about what is ahead in your reading? What are you most nervous about being challenged to do?

2. How does the pace of everyday life or cultural pressure lead you to neglect God's mission?

3. Is there an area of your life you already know is out of step with God's mission? Are you willing to make adjustments to be more fully obedient?

CHAPTER 1

Am I Really Responsible for the Whole World?

When they saw him [Jesus], they
worshiped, but some doubted.
Matthew 28:17

This generation of Christians is responsible
for this generation of souls.
Keith Green, musician

I am obligated both to Greeks and barbarians,
both to the wise and the foolish.
Paul, Romans 1:14

I WILL NEVER FORGET the day I got a call from a denominational leader from Minnesota. It is not an exaggeration to say this phone call changed my life. Until then, I had been serving in a comfortable pastorate in a small town in Alabama. I had a house on a golf course, two healthy kids, two cars in my garage, and by any measure of success, a solid ministry in a rural town. But everything changed when I answered the phone.

After a brief introduction, this brother began to talk about the needs of his convention that covered two states, Wisconsin and Minnesota. He talked about cities that were three or four times the size of the city in which I currently served; these cities had no healthy churches. As the conversation progressed, he asked if I would be willing to consider leaving Alabama to serve in these states as a pastor and church planter.

To be honest, though I had been to seminary and currently served on the Alabama State Board of Missions, this was the first time I had grasped the need for church planting and the depths of lostness in the United States. The only church planting I knew anything about resulted from churches splitting. Also, most of the lost people I knew had some knowledge of Christianity but were simply living in rebellion. The idea that so many people had so little knowledge of the gospel was mind-blowing. I was undone emotionally.

That night I talked to my wife, and we determined to put it before the Lord. We began to ask him to send us to a place where Christianity was not oozing from every pore of society. We did not know what else to do, so we bought a map of the U.S. and stole a pink crayon from my daughter's art box and marked out areas in the U.S. we thought were more Christian. Our prayer was for God to send us outside the pink places. In time, as we prayed, the Lord showed us that our map of the United States was too small. We learned about unevangelized countries and unreached people groups.

Our comfortable life had been upended, and we could no longer be content with the status quo. Our response to this calling led us to spend the better part of the next decade overseas, working with unreached peoples and serving alongside some of the greatest missionaries on the planet. Eventually we returned to the United States, not walking away from this missionary calling but expanding it by teaching missions in a Baptist seminary and mobilizing students and churches to more fully engage in God's great work around the world. It has been an unimaginable journey that started when I answered a simple phone call.

OKAY, BUT CAN I REALLY BE PART OF GOD'S MISSION?

It is easy to assume everyone who is an effective evangelist or every missionary serving on the mission field is sinless, full of faith, and extremely spiritual. When we think about what it takes to witness to our friends and family or when we try to imagine living in a different country, we cannot believe God could use someone like us in this task. We know ourselves too well—our weaknesses, temptations, lack of faith, and even areas of secret disobedience. To be fair, it is my experience that most Christians genuinely want to be faithful to God but do not believe it is even possible. We want to tell others about Jesus. We want them to have the same hope we experience. But the thought of our being God's mouthpiece seems like an unreasonable dream.

I started this chapter with the story of my call to missions because I want you to understand that, even though I am writing this book and have been part of training and sending hundreds of men and women overseas in the past two decades, this is not the path I started walking down. In fact, by most standards, I was a poor missionary candidate.

In the first conversation with our missionary consultant, this man asked if we knew what "people group" we wanted to work with. At that point I had never heard that phrase, but not wanting to appear ignorant or to embarrass myself, I answered with full confidence, "I think we'd like to work with lost people." He smiled and kindly informed us that was the only kind of people missionaries worked with. He was asking me a different question, and I didn't even know it.

The point here is, even though God's vision for each of our lives includes sharing the gospel with those who are lost and participating in his global mission, most of us are too intimidated to know how to respond. Then again, the fact that you picked up this book and have continued reading means you probably want to be more involved than you currently are. Don't let your sense of inadequacy or lack of training deter you. If you are a bit intimidated and uncomfortable, you are in good company. My guess is that, just like Frodo Baggins, everyone reading this page (including the one typing) is a bit unnerved by the daunting task before us.

Thank you for showing up and please keep reading!

THE NOT SO BRAVE DISCIPLES

When we get to the end of the Gospel of Matthew, we read some of the most amazing and faith-inspiring stories in the Bible. We learn about the resurrection of Jesus from the dead, which includes an earthquake and an angelic vision. We also see the women meeting and worshipping the risen Christ before he sent them to tell the disciples Jesus was alive. All this precedes Jesus's last words commanding his followers to make disciples of all nations and his promise to be with them until the end of the age. What an amazing crescendo to this fantastic book.

However, tucked into these sweeping narratives is an often-overlooked phrase that, when fully considered, provides a deeply human element to these miracle stories. Go back and read Matthew 28:17: "When they saw him, they worshiped, but some doubted."

You might want to look at that again to make sure you don't miss the final words: *some doubted.* If this phrase isn't confusing enough, when Mark described the scene at the end of his Gospel, he says the apostles "were afraid" (Mark 16:8). There you have it: these men are standing in the presence of the risen Christ, and he is about to charge them to take his message of salvation to the entire world. We also know, because we have read the book of Acts, that these men eventually turn the world upside down with their bravery and missionary zeal. But at this moment, they are paralyzed with fear and doubt.

Jesus promised he would rise again from the dead; the disciples had received the message that he was indeed alive, and now he was standing in their presence. Bible scholar Donald Hagner notes, "The reader is accordingly unprepared for the last three words of the verse."[1] This observation feels like an understatement. We expect celebration and worship, not hesitancy and doubt. An early church father, John Chrysostom, reminded his hearers that the inclusion of verse 17 should encourage us because it is a reminder that "even up to the last day, they were determined not to conceal even their own shortcomings."[2] Let us not forget, Matthew was there! It is safe to assume this is his firsthand account of his emotional state, as well as of those with him.

What are we to make of the inclusion of the disciples' fear and doubt in the Great Commission story? On the one hand, it reminds us of the difficulty these men had understanding who Jesus was. On the other hand, this passage serves as a reminder that these men were human, just like each of us. Sure, these men would become heroes of the faith, but at this moment their humanity was on full display. In short, this description of the disciples' shaken emotional state means that none of us should discount ourselves as missionary material. When you think about telling others about Jesus, do you feel a pang of fear? Welcome to the club.

Over the years, I have listened to well-meaning people use phrases like, "I admire missionaries, but I could never do what they do. I am too . . . ," as if missionaries are so much different. It does not matter how they complete the sentence; the meaning is the same. Fear and doubt have taken over their thinking. They fear they would not survive in a foreign country, or they fear they are not smart enough to learn another language, share the gospel effectively, or endure hardships. These fears become excuses that expose our doubt about God's call, his sustaining presence, or even the truthfulness of the gospel message itself.

As we consider these excuses, it is also important to reflect on the disciples as they stand before the resurrected Christ. These men do not deny their human emotions; but they also do not allow these emotions to determine the validity of their calling or of the fact that this calling pushed them out of their comfort zone and into the world. Instead, Matthew reminds us that, even though they doubted, the disciples also *worshipped.* Fear and doubt are powerful emotions; however, one sure way to overcome them is with a heart of worship.

C. S. Lewis provides a helpful discussion about worship in *A Reflection on the Psalms.* In this work, he tells the story of the early days of his conversion. He was particularly bothered by the constant refrain in the Scriptures requiring people to "praise the Lord." He likened this command to that of an insecure dictator requiring people to continually tell him how great he is. However, after more reflection, Lewis soon realized Christian worship is something entirely different. Christians do not worship as a meritorious act or a form of compliment and approval; rather, Christian worship is the "appointed consummation" that completes the enjoyment. "Men spontaneously praise whatever they value."[3] In other words, worship is the natural overflow of the awe and joy we experience as we grow in our knowledge and experience of God.

Lewis takes this understanding one step further by observing. "The delight is incomplete till it is expressed."[4] It is not enough for a child of God to be consumed with God's wonder and glory. This passion also compels us to express it to others. Like a man on a beach pointing out the beauty of the sunset to whoever is nearby.

> To see what this doctrine really means, we must suppose ourselves to be in perfect love with God—drunk with, drowned in, dissolved by that delight which, far from remaining pent up within ourselves as incommunicable, hence hardly tolerable, bliss, flows out from us incessantly again in effortless and perfect expression, our joy is no more separable from the praise in which it liberates and utters itself than the brightness of a mirror receives is separable from the brightness it sheds.[5]

This kind of worship overcomes fear and doubt. It compels us to tell others here and over there. When we remember all Christ has done for us, we cannot really be silent. When we consider the hopeless plight of the countless millions who live without a relationship with God, we cannot be content. When we cry out in prayer, "Someone needs to do something about this!" We come to the profound truth—"I am somebody!"

The apostles who received the original commission to make disciples of all nations serve as the headwaters of the church. What Jesus said to them on the mountain, he says through them to us, as well to each future generation. Every person who has trusted Jesus as Savior is a participant in his mission. We were first the beneficiary of the commission when someone told us about Christ; now we are responsible to obey the words of our Lord.

GOD'S SPECIFIC CALL TO MISSIONS

William Booth, the founder of the Salvation Army, is rumored to have said:

> "Not called!" did you say? "Not heard the call," I think you should say.
>
> "Put your ear down to the Bible, and hear Him bid you go and pull sinners out of the fire of sin. Put your ear down to the burdened, agonized heart of humanity, and

> listen to its pitiful wail for help. Go stand by the gates of hell and hear the damned entreat you to go to their father's house and bid their brothers and sisters and servants and masters not to come there. Then look Christ in the face—whose mercy you have professed to obey—and tell Him whether you will join heart and soul and body and circumstances in the march to publish His mercy to the world."[6]

When considering our responsibility for the Great Commission, one of the first questions asked relates to God's call. For some, this discussion is used as an excuse for not doing anything of note. For others, it is a sincere question about God's will and a desire to be obedient.

For this reason, as we continue our reflection on the Great Commission, it is important to consider the missionary calling. After all, the world is a big place, and the task of making disciples is expansive. Perhaps you are genuinely concerned about God's will, and you want to make sure you are being fully obedient. Maybe you sense God leading you into some type of ministry, but you are not sure what to do next. This section is designed to explain what is meant by the notion of being called by God. Also, you will find some guidelines for understanding and responding to God's call in your life.

Before we go further in this study, let me offer a bit of caution. What you will read below is like any tool. Used properly, it can help you build a life of faithful obedience. However, you could use these guidelines as an excuse, reasoning that God's will for you is to stay comfortably where you are now. If this is your temptation, before reading further, I recommend rereading the previous section. One key for discerning God's will and the personal implications of God's missionary call is remembering each of us has a part in God's global mission; no one is exempt. The purpose of this section is to encourage you to prayerfully consider how you can be more personally involved.

The notion of *calling* is fairly common in daily conversations. When we experience the work of an artist—whether a musician, author, or painter—we often say, "This person is fulfilling his calling." We use similar language when we refer to the sacrifice required of a successful athlete, a politician, or a businessperson. In this context, *calling* refers to passion or skill. It is often used as a label for extreme talent or commitment. However, when we use *calling* in the context of missions or ministry, we mean something different.

For the believer, the idea of calling points away from ourselves. Rather than emphasizing personal passions and talents, a Christian understanding of calling points to the one who calls. Christian calling is a description of what we experience when God takes the initiative and reveals his will to us. He calls, and our obedience to this is the only reasonable response. The passion, talent, and tenacity that result from this experience are realized as we look to the Lord for help, not from looking within. My hope is that you will begin to think about your entire life as a response to God's will. For some readers, obedience to this call will mean you will begin using different standards for evaluating daily decisions; other readers will discover obedience to God's call will demand a more radical change.

As we consider what the Bible teaches, the first and perhaps most important truth to embrace is *God calls every Christian to salvation and to service.* The Bible is clear that, left to our own sinful selves, none of us would choose or seek a relationship with God (see Rom. 3). Sure, we might want some of the benefits a relationship with God provides—hope, forgiveness, purpose, salvation—but without Christ, we are spiritually dead and would not seek these answers in God. This means, if you are a Christian, you have responded to God's call to salvation.

The call to salvation includes God's call to serve. Consider Paul's warning to the Christians in Galatia: "For you were called to be free, brothers and sisters; only don't use this freedom as an opportunity for the flesh, but serve one another through love" (Gal. 5:13). This passage reminds us that even though there are great personal benefits in the gospel, Christians are not called to simply enjoy these blessings for ourselves. In Christ, we have been set free to love and serve others. We serve those in our neighborhoods, at our jobs, schools, or wherever God sends us. We do so as part of the great commandment: loving God and loving others as we love ourselves (see Matt. 22:34–40). And we serve in obedience to the Great Commission—making disciples of all nations.

This leads us to the second important point related to the call of God. *God calls some Christians to specific tasks, ministries, and places.* This call to a specific ministry should not be considered exceptional or unique; instead, it always fits within the more general call to salvation and service. When we read the Bible and biographies of those who serve in ministry or on the mission field, we quickly become aware that God has indeed chosen some for a more specific ministry as part of his church and kingdom.

Through the years, I have come to believe that embracing this specific calling is vital for missionary endurance. In the face of difficulties, complexities, and even hostilities, the firm conviction of God's call enables one to stay and continue to serve. My wife often talks about how difficult the early months of our missionary term were for her. Everything was hard, the weather was bad, and our kids were struggling. At times, it was as if God were silent as she prayed and read her Bible. Now, when she retells the story, she says, "The only thing that kept me on the field in those early days was the firm conviction that the last clear word I had from the Lord was to go. I knew if I left, it would be disobedience." This is the power of the missionary call.

With this in mind, you may ask, "How can I know if God is calling me?" or "How can I know what God is calling me to do?" While this can be a deeply personal experience, we can divide the journey to this answer into three key components:

(1) an internal conviction, (2) an external affirmation, and (3) practical opportunities. In other words, discerning God's call will include these three experiences. Though I describe this in a certain order, you may experience these in any order. I am not prescribing a step-by-step plan for knowing the will of God; rather, I want to give names to experiences so you can better discern God's activity in your life.

Internal Conviction

God's specific calling includes a deep personal conviction that something is not right and needs to be addressed. For a missionary, this includes an uncomfortable awareness that billions of people are living and dying without adequate knowledge of the gospel. The knowledge of vast lostness may come through a sermon, a podcast, a conversation with missionaries, a book, or some other seemingly random experience. No matter how it comes, the individual is gripped by an internal conviction that captures the imagination and grows over time. Like a song you can't get out of your head, this conviction becomes a consuming thought you cannot ignore, and you know you must do something about it. This conviction becomes part of your prayer life. In Bible reading, sermons, or other studies, this theme jumps out and commands your attention. You cannot shake the notion that God is speaking to you about something important.

External Affirmation

A second experience that helps in discerning God's call happens when other people affirm or encourage you to consider a particular ministry. Perhaps someone affirms a gift or skill they see in you. Maybe you talk with a trusted friend or spiritual mentor about the growing internal conviction, and they confirm you might be perfect for this ministry. Other times, others take the initiative and ask, "Have you ever considered . . . ?" While we can't base our discernment of God's will exclusively on the opinions of others, as our internal conviction and external affirmation line up, we can be sure things are moving in a certain direction.

The Bible is clear that God guides through the wisdom of others as well as through our own personal feelings. This pattern is clearly demonstrated in the opening verses of Acts 13: "Now in the church at Antioch there were prophets and teachers: Barnabas, Simeon who was called Niger, Lucius of Cyrene, Manaen, a close friend of Herod the tetrarch, and Saul. As they were worshiping the Lord and fasting, the Holy Spirit said, 'Set apart for me Barnabas and Saul for the work to which I have called them.' Then after they had fasted, prayed, and laid hands on them, they sent them off" (vv. 1–3).

In this account, the Holy Spirit leads the elders of the church in Antioch to send Barnabas and Paul as missionaries. There is no question Barnabas and Paul had missionary hearts; after all, they had come to Antioch as missionaries. However, the affirmation they received from other church leaders seems to have served as the significant moment for these men discerning God's call.

Discerning God's will is one reason it is important to be in deep relationship with other believers. It is also important to discuss openly what you believe God is teaching with trusted mentors, pastors, family members, or other mature believers. Seek godly council and be willing to hear the call of God through the wisdom of others.

Practical Opportunities

A third crucial element for discerning God's call comes as we take part in ministry opportunities. Many Christians make the mistake of assuming discernment of God's will comes through personal meditation in a quiet place. This quiet moment can be the starting point, but a fuller understanding of God's call will come through being personally involved in hands-on ministry.

Doing ministry or serving in a particular area can generate a sense of joy and excitement that confirms what you have been sensing God doing in your life. This does not mean you perform these ministries flawlessly or there is no fear or doubt. Remember, calling is not mediated through human competencies. Instead, as you do ministry, you experience a deep sense of confirmation from the Holy Spirit.

This is one of the benefits of short-term mission trips or other ministries that push you to venture outside your comfort zone. In these moments, the Lord births in you a deep sense of dependency on him and an affirmation of his will. A holy imagination takes over and you see yourself doing this kind of thing long-term.

The opposite may also be true. It is possible that as you engage in certain ministries, you sense, *This isn't for me*. This is fine too. Your step of obedience is God's tool for guiding you. Don't make the mistake of believing you can discern God's will through inactivity, hoping for complete clarity before you act. The better way is to serve, allowing God to open doors and lead the way.

As noted earlier, one could use these tools as an excuse to do nothing. Some might say, "Well, I don't feel any conviction, and no one has asked me to do anything. God must not be calling." This would be a mistake. Rather than starting from a position of inactivity, begin with the Isaiah prayer: "Here I am. Send me" (Isa. 6:8). My friend Danny Akin, president of Southeastern Seminary, is famous for saying: "Don't ask God, 'Why should I go?' Instead, ask him, 'Why should I stay?'"

If you genuinely want to know God's will for your life, I hope these markers offer some insight into your next steps. As you join God in his mission and experience the natural difficulties that accompany any ministry, your deep-seated confirmation of God's calling may serve as your strength and source for endurance.

BUT IT ISN'T MY GIFT

Have you ever thought, *I know I should be more intentional about sharing the gospel with my friends and family, but I'm just not gifted.* This thinking is common, and it is tempting to want to delegate something as important as eternity to a professional, or someone who seems to have a special gift from the Lord. However, the Bible is clear that each of us can (and should) share Christ. Consider Jesus's words to his followers: "But you will receive power when the Holy Spirit has come on you, and you will be my witnesses in Jerusalem, in all Judea and Samaria, and to the ends of the earth" (Acts 1:8). Success in evangelism is not dependent on courage or gifting; it is rooted in the powerful presence of the Holy Spirit who indwells each of us as believers.

Through the years, as I have talked with people about their participation in missions or personal evangelism, some have countered with the notion that they would like to do so, but they do not have "the gift of evangelism." This response is interesting because even though the New Testament gives several different lists of spiritual gifts, no writer includes evangelism in the list. They mention sign gifts and service gifts;

they describe leadership gifts and ministry gifts, public gifts, and private gifts. But not one time is evangelism included as a spiritual gift.

The closest any list comes to including evangelism as a gift is Ephesians 4:11, and though some have pointed to this verse to support the claim that evangelism is a gift, a more accurate reading recognizes that Paul is calling individuals as gifts to the church rather than describing specific spiritual gifts. According to Paul, God gives the church evangelists so that the saints can be equipped for the task of evangelism. Consider these words of John Stott: "Since all Christians are under obligation, when they have an appropriate opportunity, to bear witness to Christ and his good news, the gift of an 'evangelist' . . . must be something different. . . . It must relate in some way to an evangelistic ministry, whether in mass evangelism, personal evangelism, literature evangelism, film evangelism, radio and television evangelism, musical evangelism or in the use of some other medium."[7] These individuals are indeed God's gracious gifts to the body of Christ. However, their special ministry should not be used as the reason for the rest of us to neglect the responsibility of sharing Christ.

What we mean when we think of evangelism as a gift usually describes someone who possesses an outgoing personality, an extrovert who is comfortable talking to strangers. Sadly, this misunderstanding leads most of us to assume we cannot serve God as we are. We believe our obedience requires us to transform into someone else to be more useful for fulfilling the Great Commission.

This is not the case. When we allow our perceived limitations to serve as an excuse for not sharing the gospel, we need the same reminder God gave Moses: "Who has made man's mouth? . . . Is it not I, the LORD?" (Exod. 4:11 ESV) Rather than searching for the mystical advantage of a spiritual gift, trust God. He created you, and he called you as you are for his purpose and glory.

Sure, evangelism is hard. But you can do it. Think of all the difficult things you have learned to do in your life.

You learned to drive.

You learned to do algebra.

You learned to cook.

You learned to remodel a room or tile a floor.

You learned a new language.

You even learned to order a complicated coffee beverage at Starbucks!

The fact is you do hundreds of things every week you had to learn to do. Some of them were scary or complicated when you started out. Now these activities require little thought. Why should evangelism be any different? In fact, evangelism should be more natural because, according to Acts 1:8, we do it in the power of the Holy Spirit. You see, evangelism is not a gift; it is a calling and the natural overflow of God's presence and activity in our lives.

We started this chapter asking the question, "Am I really responsible for the whole world?" The honest answer is no. However, each of us is responsible for obedience to Jesus's Great Commission. We each have a clear word through the Scriptures and a calling that is as specific as the Lord has revealed. As we continue this journey through the Great Commission, take a few moments to ponder these words from Robertson McQuilkin: "When all has been said that can be said on this issue, the greatest remaining mystery is not the character of God, nor the destiny of lost people. The greatest mystery is why those who are charged with rescuing the lost have spent two thousand years doing other things—good things, perhaps—but have failed to send and be sent, until all have heard the liberating word of life in Christ Jesus. The lost condition of human beings breaks the Father's heart. What does it do to ours?"[8]

DISCUSS AND REFLECT

1. How does the reminder that Jesus's disciples were not spiritual giants encourage you?

2. Have you ever given serious consideration to God's call on your life? Would you be willing to change your prayer from "God, why should I go?" to "God, why should I stay?"

3. If evangelism is a matter of obedience, not gifting, what is your next step in evangelistic obedience?

CHAPTER 2

By What Authority Do We Go?

All authority has been given to me in heaven and on earth. Go, therefore, . . . And remember, I am with you always, to the end of the age.
Matthew 28:18–20

Now think a moment of these words "all power." . . . We cannot grasp it; it is too high, we cannot attain unto it. Such power of self-existence, the power of creation, the power of sustaining that which is made, the power of fashioning and destroying, the power of opening and shutting, of overthrowing or establishing, of killing and making alive, the power to pardon and to condemn, to give and withhold, to decree and to fulfill, to be, in a word, head over all things.

A man who has power of all things . . .
without exception is to be obeyed by
all creatures, great and small.
Charles Spurgeon, "The Power
of the Risen Saviour"

ONE OF THE MOST inspiring missionary stories in print is the firsthand account of Brother Andrew's ministry smuggling Bibles and other Christian literature into countries where missionary work was illegal and conversion to Christianity could be punished by torture and imprisonment, even death. In his book *The God Smuggler*, Brother Andrew writes about driving his Volkswagen across closed borders while praying God would blind the eyes of guards, and he did.

The book has been translated into more than forty languages, including the languages of countries he originally smuggled Bibles into. As thrilling as these stories are, all of this work was illegal. This fact should lead us to ask the question, "By what authority do missionaries like Brother Andrew choose which laws apply to them?" After all, Romans 13 makes clear that Christians are supposed to live in submission to the laws of the land. As he contemplated God's call on his life and the implications, Brother Andrew determined that he had to live in full obedience to God rather than man or submit to the comforts of this world. With one simple prayer, he placed his life in God's hands and at God's disposal: "Whenever, wherever, however You want me, I'll go. And I'll begin this very minute. Lord, as I stand up from this place, and as I take my first step forward, will You consider this is a step toward complete obedience to You? I'll call it the step of yes."[1]

Brother Andrew's life provides a clear demonstration of what God can do when someone determines to obey him fully. When questioned about his decisions, he emphasized that it was always right to obey God rather than man. By whose authority did he perform his ministry? The authority of Jesus through the Great Commission.

ALL AUTHORITY IS GIVEN TO ME

As we continue our journey through the Great Commission, we come to Jesus's self-identifying statement: "All authority has been given to me." Anyone who reads this sentence should recognizes that what follows must be accepted with utmost seriousness. As C. S. Lewis reminds us in *Mere Christianity*, Jesus is either a liar, a lunatic, or the Lord. That is, his teachings are either untrue and he knows it, in which case he is immoral and cruel. Or Jesus is deranged or unstable, thinking he is someone he is not, in which case we should ignore him. Or what he says is true, in which case he is the all-powerful King of the universe.[2] If this is true, the only reasonable response is surrender, not negotiation.

It is probably safe to assume you would not be reading this book if you believed Jesus was either a wicked liar or an unhinged lunatic. With this in mind, let's look more deeply into this massive claim: "All authority has been given to me." What does this mean, and what impact does this truth have on the meaning of the Great Commission? To find the answer to this question, we need to look back in our Bibles into the Old Testament, specifically to the book of Daniel.

In Daniel 7, we read about the unfolding of God's plan for redemption and his undoing the destructive consequences of human sinfulness. According to E. W. Heaton, "It would be no exaggeration to say that this chapter is one of the most important passages of the OT."[3] Bible scholars agree that this vision provides insight into the rise and fall of earthly kingdoms and the ultimate establishment of God's eternal kingdom.

In the first eight verses of the seventh chapter, Daniel writes about four huge beasts coming out of the sea in rapid succession. Each beast seems more formidable than the previous. After describing the rise and fall of these earthly powers, Daniel introduces the reader to a new character:

> Suddenly one like *a son of man*
> was coming with the clouds of heaven.
> He approached the Ancient of Days
> and was escorted before him.
> He was given dominion
> and glory and a kingdom,
> so that those of every people,
> nation, and language
> should serve him.
> His dominion is an everlasting dominion
> that will not pass away,
> and his kingdom is one
> that will not be destroyed.
> (Dan. 7:13–14, emphasis added)

We know Jesus used the title "Son of Man" throughout the Gospels to refer to himself, and there can be little doubt Daniel's prophesy is a vision of the promised Messiah. Equally fascinating is the phrase in verse 14, "He was given dominion." Reading this through the lens of Jesus's earthly ministry drives our memory to similar words found in the Great Commission when Jesus tells his disciples that all authority (dominion) has been given to him.

New Testament scholar Ben Witherington notes Jesus's words in Matthew 28, intentionally highlighting himself as the one "enthroned as the ruler of the world by his resurrection which is also his exaltation."[4] In other words, with the statement, "All authority has been given to me," Jesus was doing so much more than reminding his disciples he was their boss. This declaration, harkening back to Daniel's prophesy, served as Jesus's self-identification that through his death and resurrection he claimed the role of King whose kingdom would endure for eternity.

As we continue reading Daniel's prophecy, we see the everlasting kingdom is populated with people from "every people, nation, and language" (Dan. 7:14). Each of the earlier kingdoms seems to have been individual nations that rose to power and were conquered; however, the Son of Man's kingdom is both eternal and global. He is King over all kings and the King of the world.

This reference to people from "every people, nation, and language" draws our attention back to Matthew 28. Jesus's claim of authority is followed by the word "therefore." Leon Morris notes: "We might have expected that this [the claim of authority] would lead on to his disclosure of some of the ways in which that authority would be exercised, but instead Jesus goes on to its implications for those who follow him. Therefore leads on to the fact that this has consequences for those who follow him here on earth."[5] What are these consequences? Those who follow Jesus are commissioned to "go . . . make disciples of all nations." It is as if Jesus tells his followers, "I'm the King and the nations are my citizens. Go get them and bring them into my kingdom."

It is a mistake to read the Great Commission as the "famous last words" of Jesus, as if he remembered an important fact and needed to tell someone before he disappeared. Instead, this mandate is central to God's mission that has been unveiled throughout the Scriptures. With the phrase "All authority has been given to me in heaven and on earth," Jesus is claiming the fulfillment of the Daniel prophecy; and based on this role, he is the coronated King. He is sending his people into the world on his kingdom business. We are his ambassadors, and the message and mission are for his glory and his kingdom (see 2 Cor. 5:17).

REMEMBER HE IS ALWAYS WITH YOU

In the shadow of the daunting task to take the gospel to the entire world, Jesus encourages his disciples with the eternal promise of his ongoing presence. As the disciples confront the reality of Jesus's pending departure, he reminds them that they will not be abandoned to the task. He will be with them until the end of the age. The promise of presence is one of the most important promises God ever made to his people.

- When Jacob ran for his life, fearing revenge by his brother Esau, God comforted him with the promise: "Look, I am with you and will watch over you wherever you go" (Gen. 28:15).
- When God called Moses to confront Pharaoh and release his people, God calmed his fear with the

promise: "I will certainly be with you" (Exod. 3:12).

- When the Israelites were in the wilderness, God drew them to himself with the promise: "I will also meet with the Israelites there, and that place will be consecrated by my glory. . . . I will dwell among the Israelites and be their God" (Exod. 29:43, 45).
- When the psalmist considers the darkness of this world, he is reminded: "Even when I go through the darkest valley, I fear no danger, for you are with me" (Ps. 23:4).
- The prophet Isaiah tells of God's great promise to those in trials: "When you pass through the waters, I will be with you, and the rivers will not overwhelm you. When you walk through the fire, you will not be scorched, and the flame will not burn you. . . . Do not fear, for I am with you" (Isa. 43:2, 5).
- When Jesus was born, this great promise was incarnated: "See, the virgin will become pregnant and give birth to a son, and they will name him Immanuel, which is translated "God is with us" (Matt. 1:23).

So when we read the Great Commission, it should not surprise us to see that Jesus ends with the same promise used to encourage God's people since the beginning: "And remember, I am with you always, to the end of the age" (Matt. 28:20).

It would be difficult for us to fully appreciate the significance of this promise. The disciples had spent three years with Jesus; he was a friend and a teacher. But he was much more; he was also the one in whom they had placed their trust. In the ministry timeline of Jesus's life, he taught who he was, and his death paid the penalty for sin. Now, as he wrapped up his earthly ministry, ascending into heaven, Jesus gave his followers the unimaginable responsibility of making disciples of all nations. This entire event is propped up by the timeless promise of his ongoing presence.

What does this promise teach?

First, it confirms Jesus is indeed the promised one. Though the events of the past week did not fit into their preconceived ideas about the Messiah, this promise reminded them they had not placed their faith in the wrong man. Their faith in Jesus had not been in vain. Matthew opened his Gospel appealing to the prophecy of Isaiah: "See, the virgin will conceive, have a son, and name him Immanuel"

(Isa. 7:14; see Matt. 1:23) When Jesus was born, he was literally "God with us." To underline this point, Matthew concludes his book with the same theme: Jesus will be with us "to the end of the age."

Second, this promise confirms Jesus's divinity. It is popular for skeptics and critics to argue Jesus never actually claimed to be God. They argue that later Christians made up this idea. However, this argument cannot be supported. When we read verses like the Great Commission, it is clear Jesus is reminding his followers that he is God who has come in the flesh. Who else could claim to have *ALL* authority and who else could claim to be omnipresent (meaning "present in all places at all times")? Only God! With these claims in the Great Commission, Jesus attaches himself to the divine promises in Scripture when he says, "I will be with you."

Finally, this promise points forward to the ministry and identity of the Holy Spirit. In Luke 24, Jesus gives a similar commission to reach all nations. Then he tells his disciples to wait in Jerusalem because he is about to send them "what my Father promised" (v. 49). We read a similar promise in John 16:7–11:

> "I am telling you the truth. It is for your benefit that I go away, because if I don't go away the Counselor will not come to you. If I go, I will send him to you. When he comes, he will convict the world about sin, righteousness, and judgment: About sin, because they do not believe in me; about righteousness, because I am going to the Father and you will no longer see me; and about judgment, because the ruler of this world has been judged."

These verses echo the promise made in the Great Commission. Jesus does not send his followers into the world with a mission; he goes with us and will remain with us until the end of the age.

THE PRESENCE OF CHRIST AND THE FULFILLMENT OF THE GREAT COMMISSION

Not only does the promise of Jesus's presence confirm everything we need to know about his authority and the importance of the mission. His presence should also provide us the motivation for pursuing this call. When you and I begin sharing Christ with those in our orbits or when we give serious consideration about serving on the mission field, we can expect opposition. We can expect fear. This is what led pioneer missionary David Livingstone to pray: "Send me anywhere, only go with me. Lay any burden on me, only sustain me."

If you took the time to review the stories listed earlier in this chapter, and the many other moments in the Bible when God reminded people of his presence, you'd discover they too were facing uncomfortable situations. The promise of God's presence proved to be a source of faith as well as a reason to press on with the task. This chapter has provided us a basis of authority for obedience. Now let's look at what his presence does for us and the mission itself.

First, this promise provides a calming presence. Remember the emotional state of the disciples? They were afraid and filled with doubt. As we study the Bible, we find this is common for God's children when faced with a step of obedience.

In his book *Experiencing God*, Henry Blackaby observed that when a believer becomes aware of God's leading in our lives, the next hurdle we face is a "crisis of faith." He explained this moment like this: "When God invites you to join him in his work, He has a God-sized assignment for you. You will quickly realize you cannot do what he is asking on your own. If God doesn't help you, you will fail. . . . You must decide whether to believe God for what he wants to do through you."[6] In this moment, the promise of presence can calm our fears and give us appropriate faith and courage.

Look at the first chapters of the book of Acts. In chapter 1, the apostles appear to be cowardly and confused. They ask the wrong questions and seem to shrink from action. But in chapter 2, these same men stand with boldness. Peter preaches a sermon in which he expounds the entire storyline of the Bible and calls more than three thousand people to faith in Christ. What happened? The presence of the promised Holy Spirit empowered them, comforted fear, and confirmed their faith.

Before we move on, it is helpful to remind ourselves that Jesus's promise to be with his followers to the end of the age is fulfilled in the presence of the Holy Spirit. The Christian doctrine of God is founded on the truth that we worship one God who is three persons. Jesus's promise of divine presence in the missionary task can be more clearly understood by reading

Luke's version of the Great Commission in Luke 24:44–49, as well as in Jesus's own teaching about the ministry of the Holy Spirit in John 14:15–31.

Second, Jesus's promise helps with the mission because it is a continual presence; he will be with us until the end of the age. That phrase "until the end of the age," may be a bit confusing, but it is significant. Here, Jesus reminds his followers that one day he will return physically to establish his eternal kingdom. Jesus had already taught this truth in a variety of formats—sermons, promises, parables. However, this promise assured his disciples that they would not be alone between the moments of his physical presence. Bible scholar Leon Morris writes, "He does not say 'I will be with you' but 'I am with you.' . . . In other words, the disciple is not going to be left to serve God as well as he can in the light of what he has learned from the things Jesus has commanded. The disciple will find that he has a great companion as he goes on his way through life."[7]

You and I can never be in a place geographically or chronologically in which Jesus is not also with us. This is important because the commission to take the gospel to all nations requires us to intentionally go where we will be uncomfortable. We have uncomfortable conversations. We live in uncomfortable places. Our lives are guided by uncomfortable decisions. When we cannot know where a decision will lead, Jesus promises to be there too.

Third, not only does this promise give comfort and faith in any situation and location. The promise should also remind us we are not alone in the actual work itself. This promise includes the reality of his convicting and convincing presence. Consider Jesus's promise in John 16:7–11:

> "Nevertheless, I am telling you the truth. It is for your benefit that I go away, because if I don't go away the Counselor will not come to you. If I go, I will send him to you. When he comes, he will convict the world about sin, righteousness, and judgment: About sin, because they do not believe in me; about righteousness, because I am going to the Father and you will no longer see me; and about judgment, because the ruler of this world has been judged."

Part of the ministry of the Spirit is to confirm the validity of the message he has given us. We share the truth, and he works to validate it in the hearts and minds of those we minister among.

I like to remind my students that in our evangelism and missionary activity, God works both ends toward the middle. Consider this: as a Christian, you are seeking to follow the will of God. You pray for his guidance, and you seek to live in full surrender to his will. When we live by faith, we simply trust God is acting in accordance to his will and guiding our lives.

Now, according to Jesus's promise in John 16, we also know the Lord is working in the life of the unbeliever. When crisis hits, the Lord draws the unbeliever to seek him. In times of emptiness or empty joy, the Lord exposes the vanity of life. In the face of shame and guilt, the Holy Spirit convicts of sin, righteousness, and judgment. The promise of his presence in this age means he is convicting and convincing the lost of his love and the hope in the gospel.

We started this chapter asking about authority. Who or what gives us the right to preach that Jesus is the only way to salvation. By whose authority do we pursue this mission? The answer, I hope you have seen, is that we pursue this calling by the authority of the eternal king of the universe who has promised to be with us in this life and in the life to come. It is to him that we give an account, and it is for him that we pursue the mission. John Stott said, "His authority on earth allows us to dare to go to all the nations. His authority in heaven gives us our only hope of success. And his presence with us leaves us no other choice."[8]

DISCUSS AND REFLECT

1. Reflect on Jesus's authority as the eternal King. How does this knowledge impact the way you live?

2. This chapter claims the most significant promise in the Bible is of God's ongoing presence: "I am with you." Write down three to five ways this promise encourages you.

3. What "crisis of faith" are you experiencing right now? What have you learned in this book that gives you the courage to face it right now?

CHAPTER 3

Who in the World Are We Trying to Reach?

Make disciples of all nations.
Matthew 28:19

If you go . . . consider the unreached,
consider the hardest mission fields and go
while you are young. Expect it to be hard.
Expect opposition. But persevere.
Michael Oh

Untold millions are still untold.
John Wesley

ONE OF THE FIRST friends I made when we moved overseas was a man who lived in a closed Muslim country, hostile to Christians. The only thing I knew about his people came from American news. For him it was the same: the only America he knew had been crafted by news stories in his country. We spent many hours getting to know each other, putting aside prejudices, and building a friendship that allowed us to talk about the deeper things of life.

Eventually, I was able to get a Bible in his language. I gave it to him as a gift—wrapped in paper and a bow. I was a little nervous because he had not expressed any interest in Christianity. But I will never forget the look on his face when he unwrapped the book. After carefully flipping through the pages, he looked at me and said, "I have always wanted a copy of this book. But I honestly didn't think they were available in my language."

This was the first time I had met someone who's life story included, "I have always wanted to know about Jesus, but no one has ever told me." Since that night, I have had similar experiences around the world, including in the United States; and, to be honest, it always troubles my soul to be reminded the phrase uttered by John Wesley several hundred years ago is still true in the twenty-first century: "Untold millions remain untold."

As we continue our meditation on the Great Commission, we arrive at the phrase that sets the parameters of our missionary work: "making disciples of *all nations*" (emphasis added). This phrase reminds us the gospel is good news for all people, in all times and all places. Its impact is not limited to a select few living in a single place or a single culture or single generation.

Now, when we read the English phrase "all nations," we may imagine a map or a globe and think about the lines and different colored spaces that designate the 195 countries in the world. However, the reality is, the boundaries of these countries as we know them were established by wars, peace treaties, tribal agreements, and some geographic boundaries. The fact that these lines and country names continue to change should be a clear sign that fulfillment of Jesus's Great Commission is not limited by national borders.

In fact, a closer look at the phrase in Matthew 28 gives us a clearer indication of the nature of this command. The word translated "nations" is the Greek word *ethne.* This word shares a lot of similarity with the English word *ethnic*, which highlights people who share common culture, history, or other identifiable traits. This distinction is important because it reminds us that in the Great Commission, Jesus did not focus on the lines that break up the map; rather he points us to the people who lived between those lines.

According to the International Mission Board, there are more than twelve thousand different ethnolinguistic people groups in the world. These people groups live inside and often across the normal borders of nation-states across the globe. These people groups consist of individuals who share a self-identity—language, culture, geography, history, etc. These groups make up *the nations* to which Jesus sends his disciples.

PANCAKES VERSUS WAFFLES

Several years ago, I heard an analogy that helps us understand why it is important to consider nations or people groups as the goal of the Great Commission. Consider the difference between preparing pancakes and waffles for breakfast.

With a stack of steaming pancakes on your plate, you only need to put a pad of butter in the middle of the stack and watch it melt. In time, the top is sufficiently covered. With a few flips of the stack and a couple more pads of butter, you have the whole stack properly coated. Then, when you want to add syrup, all that is needed is a random covering. The smooth top ensures that the whole stack is sticky sweet and ready to eat.

Waffles are different. Anyone who has traveled knows the experience of going into the hotel lobby for breakfast. You spread the cup of batter and across the waffle iron—close, flip, and wait. When the waffle is ready, like the pancake, it is piping hot. However, covering the waffle with butter is more complicated. It takes intentionality—paying attention to each section. If you simply dollop butter into a single square, it stays right there. The same for syrup; it only covers where we intentionally focus.

The world is not a pancake; it is a waffle. Each people group is like the square. Without intentional focus, the other squares (people groups) remain dry, devoid of the sweetness of the gospel. Christians may live geographically near an unreached people group, or the country may have strong churches or missionaries. However, this people group remains *unreached.* The International Mission Board notes that of the 12,155 people groups in the world, about 7,290 are still unreached (about 4.8 billion people). Of this group, just over 3,000 people groups (more than 280 million people) remain *unengaged*, meaning there is no strategy or gospel movement underway among them.[1]

BUT WHAT ABOUT THOSE WHO HAVE NEVER HEARD?

I will never forget sitting in a room with several new believers from a country that is hostile to Christianity. My visit was a follow-up from their baptism a day or so before. After they greeted me, I became aware of a tension in the room, and I asked what was going on.

"Is it true that a person has to believe in Jesus to go to heaven?" one of the men asked. The question caught me off guard because we had spent weeks covering the basics of Christianity.

I guess they could read my confusion because one of the men said, "We're not asking for ourselves. We believe. But we are thinking about our families. No one has ever told them about Jesus. Do they really have no other hope?"

This story should bother us. Questions about what happens to unevangelized people is more than a theological thought exercise. Faces, names, and experiences are attached to this concern. Sometimes I wish we could ignore it, but this is not possible. It is not even Christian. The consequences are too great. Millions have not heard, and the Bible is clear: unless a person hears and personally responds to the gospel, that person cannot be saved. People are not protected from the wages of sin because they have never heard. God's mercy and justice do not allow for a broader path to forgiveness through ignorance. God's grace and love were clearly displayed on the cross of Christ. As we think about the fate of those who have never heard, we need to consider a few important points.

1. People are guilty before God because of personal sin and idolatry. Many mistakenly believe that those who have never heard are innocent; however, Paul's letter to the Romans shatters this myth of an innocent unbeliever. Consider these words from the opening section of the letter.

> For God's wrath is revealed from heaven against all godlessness and unrighteousness of people who by their unrighteousness suppress the truth, since what can be known about God is evident among them, because God has shown it to them. For his invisible attributes, that is, his eternal power and

> divine nature, have been clearly seen since the creation of the world, being understood through what he has made. As a result, people are without excuse. For though they knew God, they did not glorify him as God or show gratitude. Instead, their thinking became worthless, and their senseless hearts were darkened. Claiming to be wise, they became fools and exchanged the glory of the immortal God for images resembling mortal man, birds, four-footed animals, and reptiles. (Rom. 1:18–23)

According to this passage, people are not neutral and innocent. Everyone is an idol worshipper. Because of God's creation, men and women are consumed by wonder about the world as well as experiencing inward emptiness or guilt because of sin. Neither of these experiences draws us to God; instead, humans fashion religion (or man-made worship) to eliminate guilt, or we worship created things. Both reactions violate God's first and second commandments: "Do not have other gods besides me. Do not make an idol for yourself, whether in the shape of anything in the heavens above or on the earth below or in the waters under the earth. Do not bow in worship to them, and do not serve them; for I, the LORD your God, am a jealous God" (Exod. 20:3–5).

This is why the Bible says that everyone has sinned. We have created idols, worshipped wrongly, and tried to make ourselves right with God. So, when we reflect on those who have never heard, it is crucial to reflect on each of these verses:

> Romans 3:23 says, "All have sinned and fall short of the glory of God."
>
> Romans 6:23 says, "The wages of sin is death . . ."

Those who have not heard are not right with God in their ignorance; the truth is, they are enemies of God because of what they do know and how they have suppressed it.

2. The missionary mandate and the mission impulse of early Christians highlight the foolishness of the claim that those who have never heard will be saved. If a person is free from judgment as long as they remain ignorant, then the most wicked act a person could commit would be to tell them about Jesus. If ignorance is an excuse, evangelism creates culpability. By preaching you condemn some to hell.

The problem is, even a cursory reading of the New Testament shows the first Christians were compelled to proclaim Christ to the entire world. They preached the message far and wide because Jesus had commanded them. Paul's passion was to "evangelize where Christ has not been named" (Rom. 15:20 HCSB). He sought to evangelize to the ends of the earth because he knew that God's gift of salvation placed him under obligation to those who had never heard (see Rom. 1:14–15).

It may be possible for someone who does not affirm the full authority of Scripture to embrace a broader path of inclusivism, teaching that God will save those who have never heard. But I do not believe that anyone who takes the Scriptures seriously can do so without denying significant parts of the New Testament. To do so neglects the most basic storyline of the Bible.

3. The consequences of being wrong are far too great. Philosophers refer to Pascal's Wager as a reason to believe in God. In Pascal's work *Pensèes* he describes a simple bet. To summarize, a person must bet whether God exists or not. If a person believes and God exists, she has won everything. If God does not exist, she has lost nothing. However, if she does not believe in God and he does exist, she has lost everything. The wise bet, he claimed was to believe in God.

Some argue this is a weak reason for faith in God; however it does give us some help with our question about those who have never heard. Let's see if we can use Pascal's logic on our question with a couple of "if/then" statements:

- *If* it is true that those who have never heard would not face God's judgment,
- *Then* we do no harm by aggressively obeying Jesus's commission to make disciples of all nations. Those who refuse to believe will be condemned, but those who believe will experience the joy of salvation in this world and the world to come.

On the other hand:

- *If*, as we have argued here, everyone must hear the gospel and personally call on the name of the Lord to be saved,
- *Then* a lack of obedience sentences billions to an eternity separated from God.

The consequence of believing it and behaving according to this false sense of security is simply too great.

Sometimes, when I visit places where the gospel is lacking and when people reject my witness because it is their first encounter with Christianity, I wish things were different. The numbers are so great; eternity is so long; the penalty for sin and idolatry is so severe. However, my heart and mind are captive to the Word of God, and Scripture teaches that a person must hear and place their faith in Christ to be saved.

Back to the story that opened this section . . .

The question these new believers asked literally made my stomach hurt. I didn't know what to say. However, I opened the Bible to the Great Commission and explained that Jesus had given his followers the responsibility for taking the gospel to all the peoples of the world. He wants everyone to be saved, but it is also our responsibility to obey. Then, I told them it was indeed true that the only way to be right with God was through faith in Jesus, and as of today, each of them had the opportunity to reach out to their families with the gospel. We could not change the past, but we could set a new trajectory for their future families: they could be Christians from this generation until the end of the age.

BUT WHAT ABOUT HERE IN THE UNITED STATES?

It should come as no surprise that the United States is a top destination for immigration and refugee resettlement. There are several reasons this is true: economics, safety, freedom of thought and speech—to name a few. From our missionary perspective, the presence of people from around the globe means our country holds an ever-growing population of unreached people groups, and they need to hear about Jesus.

The vast majority of refugees come from places like Myanmar, Afghanistan, Syria, Iraq, as well as a host of African nations.[2] When we think about university students who come to the United States, the majority call China and India home.[3] While we might think that the majority of those coming to the U.S. as immigrants, those wanting to settle and make a life here, are from Latin American, the largest immigration groups are from Asian countries—China, India, the Philippines.[4] What do most of these countries have in common? In a global sense, from a missionary perspective, these countries consist of unreached people groups and are hostile to Christianity and missionary activity. As we consider Jesus's commission to his church, making disciples of all nations must also include reaching those who live near us.

Over the past several years, immigration has become a cultural hot potato, dividing political parties and dominating the news cycle. There may be reasons for the concerns expressed by either side of these issues. However, from a Christian perspective, we cannot afford to be swept up in these debates and ignore the reality before us. To quote the apostle Paul in Acts 17:26, "From one man he has made every nationality to live over the whole earth and has determined their appointed times and the boundaries of where they live." Our world, and its current makeup, must be viewed through this biblical lens, trusting that the hand of the Lord is guiding events of this world for his purposes. The God of the universe is a missionary God, and he is bringing people to your neighborhood so you can tell them about Jesus.

SEEING THE WORLD THROUGH A DARK WINDOW

In 1989, Luis Bush reminded the Christian world of a section of our globe that has, historically, been resistant to the gospel: the 10/40 Window. This "window" is a rectangle-shaped area that wraps around part of the globe, from 10 degrees to 40 degrees latitude, north of the equator. Regionally, it covers North Africa, the Middle East, and South and East Asia. From west to east, the window stretches from Northwest African countries like Morocco and Mauritania to Japan and Indonesia.

Inside this window is the birthplace of every major world religion:

- Hinduism
- Buddhism
- Judaism
- Christianity
- Islam

Viewing this window through the lens of the Great Commission, we can see:

- Nearly 5.4 billion people live within this geographical window, and nearly 70 percent of the people groups are considered *unreached* people groups.[5] According to the Joshua Project: "The 10/40 Window is home to some of the largest unreached people groups in the world such as the Shaikh, Yadava, Turks, Moroccan Arabs, Pashtun, Jat, and Burmese."[6]

- The most populous countries and fastest growing/least evangelized mega-cities in the world are inside the 10/40 Window.
- According to Open Doors International, forty-seven of the top fifty countries listed with the highest degree of Christian persecution are inside the 10/40 window.[7]

If we considered the humanitarian impact of the gospel, the 10/40 Window also houses people living in significant physical crisis.

- Those living inside these countries would be considered "the poorest of the poor." Many in the region live on a few hundred dollars per year.[8] This poverty, as well as significant social and political crises, also means that those inside this window experience the lowest quality of life on the planet:
    - Highest infant mortality
    - Lowest life expectancy

- Limited literacy, access to education, and access to basic human rights

The 10/40 Window remains our world's greatest mission field. The needs are great, and it is difficult to imagine God being apathetic to this reality. My pastor often asks: "When I look at the number of unreached people in the world, and I compare it to the number of people who sense a call to missions, I have to ask, 'Is God really that bad at math?'"

Obviously, the answer is no. God has called, but the nations remain unreached. Our challenge is to listen and pray with Isaiah: "Here I am. Send me" (Isa. 6:8).

DON'T FORGET THE DARKNESS

Throughout this chapter we have discussed ideas like unreached, unevangelized, lostness, and "those who have never heard." It is easy to get comfortable with these words, and they lose all meaning and impact. Many of us have been Christians for several years. Our best friends are Christians, and most of our discretionary calendars revolve around Christian events. This is all fine and to be expected.

However, it also means we are prone to forgetting the hopelessness of life outside of fellowship with God. Before we leave this chapter, it seems necessary to take a walk down this dark road of lostness.

Perhaps the best description of life outside of Christ can be found in the first three chapters of Paul's letter to the Romans. It might help for you to take a few minutes to read through these passages, asking God to give you missionary insights into the depth and darkness of lostness. When you do, you will notice in chapter 1, Paul describes this situation in the starkest of terms:

- Under God's wrath
- Godless and unrighteous
- Suppress truth and embrace a lie—i.e., deny what you know to be true
- Idolatry
- Under God's judgment—now and eternally
- Suffering temporal consequences for sin
- Separated from God in this world and the next

The chapter ends with a reminder that those whose lives are characterized by these phrases are desperately trying to sooth their guilt and shame. Born into sin, and then behaving as sinners through active choice, people attempt to dull the senses with every level of perversion and the endless search for peace in false worship and religion. But in the end, God gives them what they want: life in sin with all its consequences.

In chapters 2 and 3, Paul continues the description by pointing out that those outside of Christ are:

- Under judgment
- Without excuse
- Dependent on God's kindness but not realizing it
- Perishing, even while they are alive
- Totally depraved, not seeking or caring about God
- Without hope of being justified before God

Brief meditation on these ideas helps us realize the desperation of life outside of Christ. This is certainly why Paul begins this segment with the reminder that the gospel is God's power for salvation for anyone who would believe (Rom. 1:16).

Charles Spurgeon, in a lecture to Sunday school teachers, pointed out they were in the business of raising the dead: "The boys and girls in your classes are, as surely as grown-up people, 'dead in trespasses and sin.' May none of you fail to fully realise [sic.] the state in which all human beings are naturally found! Unless you have a very clear sense of the utter ruin and spiritual death of your children, you will be unable of being made a blessing to them."[9]

May we never grow callous or blind to the reality of lostness or the hope available to all in Christ.

DISCUSS AND REFLECT

1. For one breakfast this week, get a plate of pancakes or waffles, and spend a few minutes praying through the lessons in this chapter about people groups.

2. Go online to https://joshuaproject.net or https://peoplegroups.org. Spend some time reading about different unreached people groups. Then add these groups to your prayer list and begin praying for them.

3. Write the story of how you came to faith in Jesus. Reflect on your life before Christ (hopeless, darkness) and spend a few minutes thanking God for saving you.

CHAPTER 4

What about Other Gods?

Make disciples of all nations, baptizing them in the name of the Father and of the Son and of the Holy Spirit.

Matthew 28:19

Even the young man who rings the bell at the brothel door is unconsciously looking for God.

Bruce Marshall, *The World, the Flesh, and Father Smith*

Many a morning have I stood on the porch of my house, and looking northward, have seen the smoke arise from villages that have never heard of Jesus Christ . . . villages whose people are without Christ, without God, and without hope in the world.

Robert Moffat, Missionary to South Africa

GANESH OWNED AN INDIAN restaurant around the corner from my apartment in Berlin. He was friendly, and over several months we developed a pretty good friendship. We talked about our families, our homes, and eventually we talked about religion. He let me know that his family had named him after a Hindu elephant god as a symbol of their devotion. I asked him if he had ever heard of Jesus, and he told me he had heard some things but he was sure the things he had heard were not true. So I followed up and asked if he had ever read the Bible. He told me he had never even seen a Bible written in his language.

I was able to get a Bible and a copy of *The Jesus Film* in his language. Several weeks later I asked how he was doing with the book and movie. He was excited to tell me that he had been reading the Bible every night and that he had watched *The Jesus Film* several times. "I even said that poem at the end of the movie." He said, referring to the prayer for salvation.

I was happy about his excitement, but I wanted to make sure we were talking about the same thing. I started asking him questions about who Jesus was and about his relationship to Jesus. "Come and see," he said as he led me into the back of his shop. "Look, Jesus is my god now too." He pointed to an idol shelf that hung from the wall. On the shelf stood an idol of the Hindu god Ganesh, a statue of the Buddha, and the boxed Jesus Film. In front of each sat a bowl of rice with a burning stick of incense.

I spent the next several months explaining that he could not simply add Jesus to his shelf of gods. For him to honor Jesus, he needed to trust him as Lord and the only God. But the more I tried to explain, the more convinced he became that more gods were better. He told me that he didn't doubt Jesus's claims but that he wanted to make sure he was covered, in case he accidentally offended the wrong spirit. To my knowledge, he never placed his trust in Jesus.

This encounter was a painful reminder that even though people are spiritual beings, religious curiosity does not lead us to the right worship of God. All efforts to appease God, get rid of our guilt, or even bask in the wonder of the universe lead to idolatry. This is the truth we mentioned in the previous chapter when we looked at Paul's writings to the church in Rome.

After claiming the gospel is God's power to save anyone who would believe, Paul pens a masterful description of the dangerous plight of humanity. He does not open this description with the emphasis on perversion. Instead, he begins with the bold statement that God's wrath is against those who "suppress the truth" (Rom. 1:18). The primary indictment of humanity is that in our natural state we create and worship idols. The entire argument in verses 18–25 revolves around the sinful human tendency to exchange "the truth of God for a lie, and [worship and serve] what has been created instead of the Creator" (Rom. 1:25).

In his famous book *Mere Christianity*, C. S. Lewis observes what he calls "the law of human nature"[1] and explains that all people are aware of right and wrong, and these same people do not live up to the standards they confess to believe. According to Lewis, this reality pushes men and women to look beyond themselves for a solution to the guilt or shame that results from the failure.

Some have mistakenly interpreted this human search for peace as the path to discover God. However, neither Lewis nor the apostle Paul makes this leap. In fact, Paul is clear that, even though there is a universal awareness of the divine and a deep-seated human need to address the guilt and shame created by conscious rebellion, "there is no one who understands; there is no one who seeks God. . . . There is no one who does what is, not even one" (Rom. 3:11–12).

How can this be?

The answer lies in the basic reality of our fallen humanity. In an effort to find solutions to the problems that plague us, our idolatrous instinct is to create a god in our own image, a god who conforms to our standards and desires. Psalm 19:1 says, "The heavens declare the glory of God." This is true; however, unregenerate people do not see God in creation. Instead, they worship creation as God. This is why Paul writes: "For everyone who calls on the name of the Lord will be saved. How, then, can they call on him they have not believed in? And how can they believe without hearing about him? And how can they hear without a preacher?" (Rom. 10:13–14). The path to salvation is not discovered through religious rituals to deal with sin. The only way a person can know God is for God to reveal himself, and his chosen vessels for revelation are the Scriptures and the witness of his people.

BUT WHAT ABOUT THE OTHER EFFORTS TO WORSHIP?

One of the main fears people express about their personal engagement in evangelism and missions is not knowing what to say or not understanding what others believe. The rest of this chapter will provide a brief overview of the basic beliefs of the major world religions and address questions of how each belief system competes with Christianity.

Now, before we get started, I want to make two important observations. First, being an effective witness does not depend on your being an expert on what other people believe. We learn about other religions in order to discover bridges and barriers[2] for evangelism. It is far more important for you to spend time studying your Bible and being an expert in your own faith. Second, this chapter will not give a complete description of other faiths. Plenty of books give a deeper look into the nuanced beliefs of others. This chapter will look at some of the key aspects of major world religions and compare them to our Christian worldview. The goal is to build confidence so you can approach anyone and any situation and share the gospel accurately and winsomely.

WORLD RELIGIONS

There are literally thousands of different belief systems in the world; however, most missiologists and scholars agree there are five primary world religions: Hinduism, Buddhism, Islam, Judaism, and Christianity. These make the list because they are both the largest faith systems and they are also found across geographic boundaries.

When we ask which world religion may boast to being the oldest, the answer most give is Hinduism.[3] This belief system does not have a single founder. Instead, Hinduism is a summary name for the varied religious traditions that developed over thousands of years throughout the subcontinent of India. Its origins can be traced back to at least 2000 BC, but it has experienced significant mutations and adaptations through the years.

Buddhism springs out of Hinduism when sometime in the fifth century BC a prince named Siddhartha Gutauma traveled outside the palace walls and faced the painful realities of life. Part of this journey included seeing "a young child full of energy and joy, and an old, decrepit man in great pain, a very sick younger man, and clearly near death, and finally a funeral procession carrying a decaying corpse."[4] The startling combination of these experiences caused him to seek answers for the meaning and purpose of life.

Culturally, Hinduism and Buddhism are rooted in South Asia. Each has a strong emphasis on meditation, idolatry, temple worship, and dietary rules. Neither faith places strict emphasis on morality; rather the goal is to live in such a way that life adheres to particular philosophies required by the worship of select deities or, at times, no god at all.

Judaism's origin story begins when a nomad named Abram received word from the Lord to leave his home and journey to a foreign land. This command came with a promise that, because of his obedience, his offspring would be as numerous as the stars and would also be a blessing to all the families of the earth. Later, the king of Egypt adopted an orphan named Moses. He was eventually exiled to the desert where he received a calling to lead Abram's descendants out of slavery to set up a nation and a more formal religion.

Many of the rituals that make up modern Judaism cannot be found in the Bible. Instead, adherents developed these practices during the years of exile along with the construction of and worship rituals of the second temple. This is the Judaism reflected in the New Testament. Strictly speaking, Judaism today is not an Old Testament faith. It is a cultural expression of a faith that developed through the years.

When it comes to the history of religion, Islam is the baby on the block. It began in the Arabian desert around the mid AD 600s when Mohammad experienced a series of visions.

At first, he assumed these were from the Satan, but his wife convinced him to take these as guidance from God. His vision was for a religion that would bring the people of Arabia out of polytheism to the right worship of one God.

Islam insists on a strictly ordered culture and society. Each person, meal, and event has a proper place in everyday life. It is an Arabic faith, meaning Islam's origin is within the Arabian Peninsula; and therefore the clothing and rituals are rooted in a Semitic context. Men and women have strict predetermined roles in religion as well as in society. Islam also places a strict emphasis on morality and religious ritual as the path to salvation.

It is popular to claim Christianity is not a religion but a relationship. Those of us who are insiders know what this statement means; however, it is also a bit short-sighted. Christianity has many significant religious elements; and, if we are going to understand our faith and understand how it compares to others, we need a similar introduction. So let's take a quick look at the basics of the faith.

Christianity's origin story begins after Jesus was raised from the dead and ascended into heaven. One of the unique elements of the faith is Jesus's regular promise that he would return to Earth again to culminate the plan of God. Before leaving, Jesus commissioned his followers to take the message of God's forgiveness through Christ to the world, and they did.

Christianity has several significant rituals—baptism, the Lord's Supper, worship services, holidays, and holy days. However, it is different from other world religions in that its founder (Jesus) claimed to be God, and throughout his ministry and teaching he regularly emphasized this claim. Also, the Christian message is firmly rooted in the belief that Jesus is still alive and will come back as Judge and King for all eternity. Believers are saved from the penalty of their own sin through faith in the substitutionary atoning death of Jesus.

According to Timothy Tennent, "The lifeblood of Christianity is found in its ability to translate itself across new cultural and geographic barriers."[5] Unlike the other religions, Christianity has proven (often through fiery trials) that its message is both relevant and life-giving in every culture.

Stanley Grenz warned, "We simply cannot allow Christianity to be relegated to the status of one more faith among others. The gospel is inherently an expansive missionary message. We believe not only that the biblical narrative makes sense for us but is also good news for all."[6] Christianity's message is that the gospel "provides the fulfillment of the longings and aspirations of all people. It embodies the truth—truth of and for all humankind."[7]

As you can see, each religion is different in origin as well as in its primary goal. In the next section we will explore some of the basic beliefs of each faith. As we noted earlier, this is not a complete description or assessment of each religion. Instead, we will focus on three primary questions:

- What does each religion believe about God?
- What does each religion believe about the purpose and goal of life?
- What does each religion teach about salvation or about the source of hope in and beyond this world.

WHO IS GOD?

Hinduism is a polytheistic faith. This simply means a belief in many gods. With respect to Hinduism, someone said Hinduism accepts the existence of more than 330 million gods. I'm not sure how it's possible to catalog this many different gods, but suffice it to say, each person/family/clan/village may worship different gods, engage different worship rituals, and follow the teachings of different holy men. Within the Hindu pantheon of gods, three stand out as primary:

1. Brahman is the impersonal creator or ultimate reality of the universe.
2. Vishnu is the preserver or protector. Vishnu is an incarnated deity who serves as a messenger of sorts. He has appeared through the years as Krishna, Rama, Buddha, even as Jesus.
3. Shiva is the destroyer.

Hinduism is a way of life and religious practices that defies simplistic descriptions. Little can be said about Hinduism that is uniformly true of all Hindus. Hinduism's flexibility can be clearly observed in its multiplicity of gods along with the many forms and goals of worship.

Buddhism is best understood as a moderated atheism. Buddha himself is reputed to have refused to acknowledge whether God existed. In fact, he did not think believing in God was important to human pursuits. During his life, the Buddha was an agnostic; however, since his death many of his followers venerate him and pray daily to statues of him. The primary difference between Hinduism and Buddhism is that the latter renders belief in God irrelevant but seeks to supply a series of teachings designed to provide a path to enlightenment, while the former is designed as the attempt to worship and please any number of gods.

Islam maintains a strict monotheism. It is the worship of and submission to a singular, divine being. Allah is completely transcendent, sharing no connection with any aspect of creation. Because of this, the goal of Islam is not to *know* Allah; instead Muslims seek to live in full submission to his will. When Muslims pray, "Allah, most merciful and compassionate," this is an acknowledgment that everything necessary for life comes from him. It is an acknowledgment of his greatness and of human finitude. His compassion is most clearly expressed in the fact that he has provided his book, the Koran, and a path of righteousness designed to fill the void of human ignorance.

Christianity also affirms monotheism—God is one. However, this basic theology differs greatly from Islam (and even from Judaism) in that we are Trinitarians. Christians affirm belief in God who exists in three persons—the Father, the Son, and the Holy Spirit. Each person is fully divine. God is Creator and therefore is transcendent (different from creation); however he is also actively involved in the events and affairs of this world. Theologians use the term *imminent* to refer to this divine quality. God is both loving and kind in his actions toward his creation. God both hears and answers prayers. He is knowable in so far as he reveals himself to us, which he has done through the incarnation of Jesus and in the Scriptures.

WHAT ARE THE GOAL AND FLOW OF HISTORY?

Both Hinduism and Buddhism affirm a cyclical/never-ending view of history. This world has no real beginning and no predicted end. The goal is for human beings to transcend through the cyclical process of reincarnation, hoping to be progressively better and eventually to achieve Nirvana, being subsumed into the ultimate reality itself. Hinduism measures the goal as good works, which enable one to progress through the Wheel of Samsara, which is a visualization of the different levels of life and death. In Buddhism, the goal is to follow a path of enlightenment, which eventually leads to a release from this world as one overcomes suffering by ending human desire.

According to Islamic doctrine, the flow of history is linear. There was a moment of creation, and at some undetermined time everything will be destroyed by fire. The world has a definite end, which includes punishment in hell for the wicked and paradise for good Muslims. While there is no assurance of salvation, Muslims hope in the mercy and good will of Allah for their future reward.

Christianity also teaches that history is linear. Everything began with God's creative act, and all history is moving toward his plan. According to the Bible, all of history is moving toward a redemptive end where sin is crushed and the kingdom of Christ is established for all eternity. The hope of Christianity is in a good God who of his own free will made a way to right the wrongs in this world as he brings new heavens and new earth into existence. This world's history will come to an end when Jesus returns and takes all of those who believe in him to be with him forever. Christianity also promises punishment for all who reject God's forgiveness in Christ. This punishment is eternal, painful, and inescapable.

WHAT MUST WE DO TO BE SAVED?

To be fair, the idea of salvation differs greatly among each of these religions. For some, the notion of being rescued or saved does not even make sense. But this section will address the ultimate goal for humans within each belief system, and we will learn what it means to be "right" in the universe or with God.

For Hindus, good works and proper ritual build good karma. This good karma makes it possible, after several (numbering in thousands or millions) reincarnations for the soul to be subsumed into the ultimate reality—free from the cycle of life and released into nonexistence. This journey is not a result of love but rather the end of a frustrating and painful human existence pursing the impersonal. Timothy Tennent has observed of Hinduism, "True knowledge . . . is eternally reverberating throughout the universe as resonating sound known as anāhata śabda (i.e., the "unstruck sound"). . . . However, there is no certainty that sages have heard—or even that it is possible to hear—the full content."[8] This allows for continual adjustment and refinement of the correct path.

Buddhism's philosophy of life is built around an eightfold path, which is the blueprint for enlightenment. The primary belief system rests on four noble truths:

1. Suffering permeates all existence.
2. Desire for anything is the cause of all suffering.
3. Suffering will cease if you suppress all desires.
4. The only way to cease all suffering is to follow the eightfold path which is a middle way between self-indulgence and self-mortification.[9]

As with Hinduism, Buddhism's hope is progressing toward Nirvana, which literally means "being blown out" or "extinguished," referring to an event or process of the extinguishing of the fires created by attachments, desires, and ignorance. In the end, these fires are put out, and the soul comes to an end as one is released from the cycle of rebirth.

Salvation in Islam rests on the will of Allah. No human has the right or knowledge to presume upon his will. Islamic life and worship are guided by five pillars of faith:

1. Confession
2. Prayer
3. Fasting
4. Alms giving
5. Pilgrimage to Mecca

Islam teaches people are separated from Allah because of ignorance, and this causes sin. Everyone is born a Muslim, but this ignorance causes us to backslide through life because of what we do not know (or remember). For this reason, life is for gaining knowledge and living in right submission to the will of Allah. Salvation is the result of diligent work and cautious living so as not to offend the will of Allah. The reward for faithful living is being released from this world for a life in paradise, which is an entirely different reality. What was forbidden in this world is now the reward of the faithful. Heaven, or Paradise, is not a place Allah dwells, and eternity does not include living in his presence or knowing him.

For Christians, salvation is not the result of human effort and does not consist of a release from this world. Instead, the Bible teaches that all people have rebelled against God and are sinners by their nature and personal choice. Because of this sinful situation, everyone is destined for eternity separated from God. But God is rich in mercy and has great love for humanity. Because of this love, God the Son became human in order to endure the full penalty for human rebellion. As a result of his suffering, human beings are now able to be right with God through faith.

The Bible teaches that when people place their faith in God's work in Christ, they are immediately declared righteous and are made a part of God's global and eternal family. He is their father and they are his children. Because of this, eternity for the believer includes life in his presence for all eternity. Heaven is described as a new heaven and earth where Christians enjoy the presence and blessing of our loving God. Hell is described as the destination for those who reject Jesus and therefore must endure eternal punishment for their own sin and rebellion.

Some who study religion make unfounded claims that the different faiths are essentially the same and that God will accept the faithful, sincere efforts of anyone. However, I think you can see through this brief discussion that this claim cannot be true. Each religion is fundamentally different. This should lead naturally to the question: How can we share Christ with those of different religions? While there is no magic formula or secret code that ensures a hearing or acceptance, here are a few helpful tips.

First, *don't make the mistake of assuming adherents of these faiths are all the same or believe the same thing.* The discussion above is intended to give you some simple handles for understanding your neighbors or for being more effective on the mission field. But at the end of the day, we are talking to real people. While it is worth knowing a little about different religions, we can also make the mistake of assuming the other person understands or believes each element of their faith as we've read about in a book. Sharing the gospel still involves relating to a person. Ask, listen, and share.

Second, *seek to be an expert in Christianity, not other religions.* Remember Paul's words: "The gospel . . . is the power of God for salvation" (Rom. 1:16). The best witness is not the person who is full of knowledge about other worldviews. The most helpful witness is growing in his or her knowledge of Christ and whose life is being transformed by the gospel.

Third, *don't give up too quickly.* Asking someone to walk away from long-held beliefs about God, the world, and salvation is a tall order. It takes patience and love. If you want some practical steps, follow these four principles:

1. Practice hospitality. Get to know people who are different from you. Invite them into your home. Include them in your holiday celebrations. Make them a part of your life so they can see how your relationship with Christ makes a difference from life apart from Christ.
2. Practice the *Golden Rule—do unto others as you would have them do to you* (see Luke 6:31). It is never right to treat others unkindly or to look for ways to be deceptive or manipulative. You would not like that, and Jesus was clear that we should treat people as we want to be treated.
3. Practice your faith in public. One of the great lies of our Western, individualistic culture is that religion is private. No other world faith accepts this as true, and neither should you. Live as a Christian in every sphere of your life.

4. Practice patience. One fact remains true—the decision to follow Christ requires several significant mental and emotional steps. We may want the other person to trust Christ the first moment we talk about him. But, as you have seen in this chapter, the basic worldviews of these beliefs are fundamentally different from Christianity. Kindness and wisdom demand that we walk slowly with people toward Jesus.

This chapter opened with a story about my friend Ganish, but I want to close with a story about my friend Mohammad. One day he found me in church and told me he had never read the Bible but would like to. The next time I saw him, he told me he had read the entire New Testament several times and had some questions. When we met together, he pulled out several pages filled with scratches, lines, and words. We spent hours working through each question until one afternoon he said, "Okay, I believe." From that day forward, he became a leader in our little house church. Every time someone had a question about how Christianity was different, Mohammad answered them, and he led several people to faith in Jesus.

One day on a train he told me that he needed to go back home to tell his family about Jesus. On the one hand, I was proud of him and excited about the possibility. However, I also knew that his openness would put his life in danger. "What can they do to me?" He smiled. "I have already died with Jesus, and I will always live with him. But, if I don't go tell my family, they can never know about this new life."

DISCUSS AND REFLECT

1. Do you know anyone from a different country? What does this chapter teach you about their religion?

2. Spend a few minutes asking God to allow you to talk with this friend about Jesus.

3. If you do not know anyone from a different country, ask the Lord to lead you to a friendship with someone so you can share Christ with them.

CHAPTER 5

What Is the Missionary Task?

Make disciples of all nations, baptizing them in the name of the Father and of the Son and of the Holy Spirit, teaching them to observe everything I have commanded you.
Matthew 28:19–20

If everything is missions, nothing is missions. If everything that the Church does is to be classified as "mission," we shall have to find another term for the Church's particular responsibility for "the heathen," those who have never yet heard the name of Christ.
Stephen Neill

The spirit of Christ is the spirit of missions. The closer we get to him, the more intensely missionary we become.
Henry Martyn

I REMEMBER DRIVING PAST a relatively large mainline church in our city reading the sign out front: *Come join our church mission trip as we tour historic sites of civil rights history.* The sign and its meaning shocked me. I was in the process of planning several short-term mission trips with seminary and college students to share the gospel among several unreached people groups. It was clear that we had two different ideas about missions.

Please understand, I am not making light of the struggle minority peoples have endured in the pursuit of a more just and equal society. I'm from the Deep South, and many of these historic sites were part of my education. There is value for Christians to be better acquainted with our nation's history in order to better love all our neighbors. However, the question plagued my mind in reaction to that sign: Can both experiences really be considered *missions*? Can the missionary task be defined with such broad and disconnected ideas? Specifically, can activities like touring historic sites—valuable though they may be—be labeled *missions* in the same way sharing the gospel is?

As we think about these questions, I'm reminded of the story of legendary football coach Vince Lombardi, whose Green Bay Packers lost the 1960 NFL Championship game to the Philadelphia Eagles. The Packers started the fourth quarter with a thirteen-point lead, but eventually lost the game seventeen to thirteen. At the start of the 1961 season, the players were greeted by a simple introductory speech that began with the phrase: *Gentlemen, this is a football.*

Coach Lombardi realized the path to success started with a clear understanding of the fundamentals of the game. The same can be said for our fulfillment of the Great Commission. Before we can obey with confidence and competence, we need to be able to answer the questions: What is missions? What is the goal of evangelism?

When we read the Great Commission in the original Greek language, the primary verb in the command is the word we translate with the phrase "make disciples." According to Craig Blomberg, this command describes "a kind of evangelism that [starts at, but] does not stop after someone makes a profession of faith. The truly subordinate participles [baptizing, teaching] . . . explain what making disciples involves. . . . The first of these will be a once-for-all decisive initiation into Christian community. The second proves a perennially incomplete lifelong task."[1]

It is a mistake to assume the primary task of missions is to convince someone to join our team. Some envision it with the same idea of national signing day for college athletes. Most sports fans are familiar with the scene—a high school athlete sits at a table lined with hats and jerseys representing the different schools who have expressed recruiting interest. As news cameras roll, the player scans the table and selects the hat from the school he plans to attend and places it on his head.

We often envision the missionary task in similar fashion, as if the goal were to get the other person to choose our team's jersey. If they are adherents of another faith, we want them to exchange their hat (or their book) for ours. However, this is not the case. This is far too simplistic. As Bloomberg noted, the Great Commission task begins with evangelism—winning them to faith in Christ. However, if we stop there at the moment of conversion, we have missed the point.

This brings us to the question, What did Jesus mean when he told his followers to "make disciples" of all nations? One might think that such an important commission would come with a more complete explanation. However, neither Jesus nor Matthew, when he recorded Jesus's words, felt compelled to provide a detailed description of the goal. I think one reason for this absence of specifics is because these eleven men had experienced disciple-making with Jesus over the past three years. In many ways, Jesus was telling them to replicate what he had done with them. David Bosch noted, "The followers of . . . Jesus have to make others into what they themselves are: disciples."[2] By eating, drinking, living, and teaching alongside these men, Jesus had made them his disciples. Now the charge is to repeat the process.

With this mandate to make disciples, Jesus is prioritizing the kingly mandate that was foreshadowed in Daniel 7:14. This prophecy included the promise that "those of every people, nation, and language should serve him." Those who have previously worshipped other gods are now called to identify with the one true God who is Father, Son, and Spirit. The commission also includes the idea of life transformation as these new disciples obey all Jesus taught. In other words, this Great Commission is a spiritual task with spiritual consequences as men and women from every nation become citizens of the kingdom of Christ.

As we consider the ramifications of the Great Commission and the core elements of our missionary task, it may be helpful to address some confusion about the idea of *kingdom work*. It is not uncommon to hear this phrase to identify good work done by well-meaning people in social, business, cultural, or governmental spaces. The phrase is often used to distinguish traditional church ministry from other seemingly good activities. This confusion creates some tension as we search for a handle for understanding missions.

It is right and good for Christians to engage in our world in meaningful ways. However, it is the concern of this book that much being done as *kingdom work* lacks any real connection with the King and his spiritual kingdom. In the words of theologian Scot McKnight: "I want to raise a red flag here: There is no such thing as kingdom work outside the church—and I don't mean the building. The kingdom is about King Jesus and King Jesus' people and King Jesus' ethic for King Jesus' people."[3]

If we set our priorities around social or cultural transformation, at the neglect of disciple-making and evangelism, our mission suffers. Though we will certainly receive accolades and applause from many outside the faith, our stated goals cannot succeed because the foundation of this world is fallen. Second, and perhaps more importantly, if these distractions lead us away from our primary missionary task, we will fail at the one ministry that God's church *alone* has been charged to accomplish.

There are many activities Christians may, and perhaps even should, participate in. However, if we do not live evangelistically and seek a mission of making disciples of all nations, then we will stumble in the only responsibility we alone can accomplish.

- Should we teach? Yes, but so do teachers.
- Should we vote? Yes, but so do millions of other citizens.
- Should we feed the hungry, clothe the naked, help the poor and the prisoners? Of course, but so do the government and nongovernmental organizations.
- Should we work for a more just society? Yes, but how many others are seeking similar goals?
- But who will tell the world about God's work in Christ and the hope that can be found in Jesus? If we fail at this point, we will have failed at our primary mission.

Many will applaud the social, cultural, and political work Christians engage in. But the work of evangelism and disciple-making will always be unpopular and will require focus and discipline. J. D. Payne does a marvelous job clarifying the confusion and highlighting the importance of keeping these aspects of the mission a priority:

> Engaging in God's mission includes caring for those with physical needs and planting churches; it involves social justice and evangelism. But here is the point of confusion. The church has wrongly assumed that since God's mission and the Church's mission are wide and diverse, then nothing is to be prioritized. All activities are equal in God's eyes, and emphasis is not to be placed on any aspect of the Church's work. An examination of the New Testament, however, reveals specific attention given to apostolic labors. . . . A prioritization was the expectation.[4]

LIVING OUT GOD'S MISSION

We have reached the point in this book where we turn the mirror and take a deep look at ourselves. Far too many Christians give an approving nod to the task of missions and evangelism without personalizing—or owning—the call themselves. In the pages that follow, we want to supply several points of application.

As I think about the principles below, I'm reminded of the process of cooking from a recipe. Sometimes when I want to make a new dish, the recipe calls for an ingredient I do not have. When this happens, two options come to mind. First, I could skip the ingredient and hope it doesn't affect the overall taste of the dish. Or second, I can look for a substitute ingredient. My hope is you won't skip over what follows because it doesn't fit perfectly within your current context. Instead, let these challenges spur your imagination as you personalize the recipe for your own missional lifestyle.

Start with a Joyful Yes

The most significant step to living out the Great Commission is for us to surrender our plans and our wishes to Jesus. He is the Lord of the mission and the Lord of our lives. His plans for us are good; and, according to Ephesians 2:10, we are his workmanship, created in Christ Jesus for good works, which God prepared ahead of time for us to do. However, far too often we want to maintain the right to say no to God's designs for us.

As we noted earlier, making the Great Commission a priority may place us in uncomfortable situations. God's call may require a change of plans or alter our life goals. Obeying God's call to missions could lead you to move, change jobs, or adjust the way you spend your time and money. Just like Jesus's challenge to the disciples on the mountain, it would have been impossible for them to reach the nations without adjustment and discomfort. On the other hand, they would also have missed out on joy and intimacy with God that is the result of a life fully surrendered to him.

Opportunities that come with my job, and the fact that my family lives in different states, require I spend quite a bit of time driving. Occasionally I'll be driving on one side of the interstate and see a major traffic jam on the opposite side. As I continue in the opposite direction, I get to a point where traffic on the other side seems to be flowing freely, but I know trouble is just ahead. Sometimes I think I'd like to tell them, "You need to turn off now. I know you can't see what's up ahead, but if you keep going, you'll be sorry."

This is how I feel at this moment in this book. Having spent the better part of the past three decades involved in missions, and sending hundreds of students to the mission field. I want to tell those who hesitate about surrendering to Jesus, "I know things seem to be going well right now, but if you say no to God right now, you are headed into trouble." Remember Jonah? You might not end up in the belly of a fish, but you will miss the joy that accompanies a life lived for King Jesus.

Begin by telling the Lord: "The answer is yes. Help me understand your call."

Prayer as a Missionary Tool

Wesley Duewel said, "We can reach the world, if we will. The greatest lack today is not people or funds. The greatest need is prayer."[5] Earlier in this book we recounted the story of William Carey and his famous sermon that sparked a missionary revolution. One of the crucial outcomes of this sermon was the establishment of the Baptist Missionary Society. This is the missionary organization that sent Carey to India. In one of the more dramatic moments of this process, Carey told his friend Andrew Fuller, "I will go down into the pit, if you will hold the ropes."[6] The same request is on the lips of missionaries today. Will you hold the ropes in prayer?

It is easy to overlook the importance of prayer. However, to do so is to neglect one of the greatest missionary tools available to us. Consider Paul's words at the end of his second letter to the Thessalonian church:

> In addition, brothers and sisters, pray for us that the word of the Lord may spread rapidly and be honored, just as it was with you, and that we may be delivered from wicked and evil people, for not all have faith. But the Lord is faithful; he will strengthen you and guard you from the evil one. (2 Thess. 3:1–3)

As Paul concludes his letter to these relatively new believers, he appeals to them for prayer. Through prayer, the church becomes a partner in the work. Paul's request gives some direction for how you can pray more effectively for missions.

First, *pray for missionary success.* Paul asks them to pray for the spread of the gospel and its reception. Each of these themes can shape how we pray. The first request is that Paul's preaching the gospel would spring legs and run. Anyone who has struggled to share Christ in a context where he is not known understands the agonizing struggle of evangelism. It often feels like the message bogged down in a pit of mud. It is exceedingly painful to watch people live in darkness when the light of the gospel is so near. So, when we pray for missionaries, we pray that the word will *spread rapidly.*

Second, *pray for a full reception of the message.* In one of the more picturesque moments in his first letter to the Thessalonians, Paul points them back to their own conversion as source material for prayer. This is how Paul describes their conversion:

> Our gospel did not come to you in word only, but also in power, in the Holy Spirit, and with full assurance. You know how we lived among you for your benefit, and you yourselves became imitators of us and of the Lord when, in spite of severe persecution,

> you welcomed the message with joy from the Holy Spirit. As a result, you became an example to all the believers in Macedonia and Achaia. For the word of the Lord rang out from you, not only in Macedonia and Achaia, but in every place that your faith in God has gone out. Therefore, we don't need to say anything, for they themselves report what kind of reception we had from you: how you turned to God from idols to serve the living and true God and to wait for his Son from heaven, whom he raised from the dead—Jesus, who rescues us from the coming wrath. (1 Thess. 1:5–10)

These men and women had experienced the full transformation that results from believing the gospel. When you think about praying for missionaries, take time to reflect on your own testimony. What change has the gospel made in your life? Did it give you hope? Did it destroy your addictions? Did it erase your shame? Did you find freedom, forgiveness, and family? These are the same needs people around the world struggle with. Pray through your own testimony when you pray for missionaries. "Pray . . . that the word of the Lord may . . . be honored just as it was with you" (2 Thess. 3:1).

Third, *pray for protection*. Paul reminds the Thessalonians that people are wicked and some stand in opposition to the gospel. Earlier in this book we learned about unreached people groups and the 10/40 Window. One of the points we emphasized was the increased persecution in these areas. Courageous missionaries have followed God's call into many of these dangerous places. We hold the rope for them by praying for their protection.

We can pray for God's protection from oppressive enemies of the gospel. However, we can also pray for the families and children of missionaries. These young people face the same pressures as our kids in the U.S., but they also face the compounded stress of different cultural pressures. In this spiritual battle, we also pray missionaries would be protected from their own temptations. The enemy loves nothing more than dragging one of God's servants into the mire of sin.

Brother Andrew reminds those of us who hold the ropes:

> We are living in what appears to be the most cruel period of history. More people suffer for the name of Christ than in any other generation. As Christians who are not under such persecution, we must find a way that we can help our persecuted brothers and sisters. They need us more than ever—our presence, our encouragement, our support, our teaching, our fellowship, and perhaps more than anything else, our prayers. Our prayers are crucial because our best praying will move us into our best actions.[7]

You might say, "Okay fine, but how do I do it? I don't know how to pray for missionaries." Here are a few quick tips.

1. *Pray for the missionaries who are connected to your church.* If your church has direct contact with missionaries, put them at the top of your prayer list. Send them a note and ask for prayer updates or specific ways you can pray for them. Let them know you want to pray through

2 Thessalonians 3:1–3, and ask for clarity on what this means in their context.

2. *Contact a mission agency and ask them about praying for missionaries.* The International Mission Board and the North American Mission Board of the Southern Baptist Convention have entire departments dedicated to helping you pray more often and more effectively for their missionaries. The same will be true for any other agency.

   It could be overwhelming to get requests from many different organizations, so pick a couple and start there.

3. *Pray for persecuted believers and unreached people groups.* The book of Hebrews reminds us to pray for those in prison "as though you were in prison with them" (Heb. 13:3). This can be a little more complicated, but the same mission organization you contact for number 2 may also be able to get you information about

unreached people groups. You could also search online for ministries dedicated to people groups and persecuted Christians. Any of these will help you with prayer prompts.

4. *Pray for yourself.* Ask God regularly how you can be on mission with him. It is important to pray for others, but it is equally important to remember you too have a part in the mission. My pastor frequently reminds us: "You need to put your yes on the table, and let God put it on the map."

Do Something on Mission—Turn Your Yes into Action

I've heard that most football stadiums are filled with thousands of fans in the stands who are in desperate need of more exercise surrounding several dozen men on the field who need rest. This may or may not be completely accurate, but it does emphasize a point that applies to missions. Most people in the church would be "fans" of missions. That is, we think telling others about Jesus is a good thing. We celebrate those who are courageous enough to step out and be involved in personal evangelism or missionary activity. We are even willing to give a little money to the cause when asked. However, few of these "fans" ever actually step onto the field. We are content to give our approval and applause, but never our own effort. But if we take seriously that the Great Commission is for all of us, then Jesus never intended for missions to be a spectator sport. In this section, we are going to explore several activities designed to move you from fan to missionary.

1. Design a mission plan for your daily life. Many of us have been around companies or other organization while they are developing mission statements and strategies. These exercises are designed to help leaders and employees know how to determine what is most important as well as what to say no to. This same exercise could be helpful for you. Rather than simply going with the flow of life, letting people and opportunities pass you by without any sense of mission, let's begin to see our lives as a mission field and make plans to live on mission wherever God leads.

Write down the different places you frequent in an average week. Just like a missionary who serves in an international setting, it is crucial for you to understand your context.

- Family
- School (yours or your kid's)
- Neighborhood
- Work
- Hobbies and kid's activities

What makes each of these places unique? What opportunities exist in each of these spaces that create open doors for talking about Jesus? Are there particular barriers or hindrances in these spaces that make it more complicated to be on mission? What could you do to take advantage of these opportunities or overcome barriers? Be creative and courageous. You aren't committing to anything yet.

Make a list of people you know who don't know Jesus, or who you are not sure are believers. It may be helpful to look at your list above (places you go) and think about specific people you interact with in these spaces. Be specific—think of specific names and faces. Write them down. It isn't helpful to think, *Everyone at work.* Or, *All the parents of my son's baseball team.*

Next to each person jot down what you know about their spiritual life. Do they worship another God? Are they too distracted by life to think about God? Are they bitter or hurt? What do you think their next step toward Jesus would look like:

- More information?
- A compassionate Christian friend to share life with?
- A challenge to get serious about spiritual matters?
- Help with a specific question?

Make a plan to start your life as a missionary where you live. In each space, and with each person, be alert for open doors of ministry. Listen for conversation topics and open doors. Make specific plans to create missional opportunities.

Here is an example that may spur your missional imagination. I know a young man who is a firefighter. He and a buddy began thinking about the different struggles first responders face each day and how their own relationships with Jesus helped them. As they prayed together, they had the idea of starting a Bible study and prayer group specifically for first responders between shifts.

After several weeks of praying, they approached the captain to ask for permission to use one of the training rooms. He agreed. They then had to decide what to teach; neither had any formal training in the Bible. The decided they would invite these men and women to watch a series of online videos and then open the floor for discussion.

The first week, the room was full of first responders. Many had no interest in attending church, but in a room of like-minded people, they felt safe asking challenging questions and exploring the faith. The room was filled with men and women who had participated in the worst days of people's lives. The conversations are not always peaceful, and no topics were off limits. These young men saw a spiritual need and knew their brothers and sisters in the department needed Jesus. They also believed God had placed them in a certain context as his missionaries.

2. Join with others on mission, and invite others to join you. You should not feel singularly responsible for every missionary venture you participate in. God has placed you in a community of believers. You are part of a local church. In your city, there must be ministries run by Christians, helping different groups of people. We all know there is more joy and productivity when Christians share the load. Perhaps your next step is to find where others are engaged in God's mission and join in. Here are a couple of ideas.

Go on a short-term mission trip. Over the years, mission trips have gained a bad reputation. They are expensive and often fuel a sense of consumerism for the traveler. Some represent poor missionary practice and foster unhealthy dependency or even promote bad examples of Christianity. However, when these trips are well planned and executed, the benefits far outweigh the issues.

Mission trips help us envision ourselves in cross-cultural settings. I have been leading students on trips for nearly twenty years, and it never ceases to amaze me to see how often God confirms a call to missions through the experience. Before the trip, these young people have an idea that missions may be cool. But since the entire notion is "foreign" (pun intended), they find it easy to compartmentalize the calling. But, on location, they realize God can use them, and they can imagine doing this for longer periods of time.

Mission trips can also help the missionaries and encourage local Christians. The best mission trips are planned in partnership and consideration of the goals and plans of those on the mission field. We work together and can accomplish tasks, events, and projects that would have been impossible without outside help.

If your church does not have any mission trips planned, take the initiative. Talk with your pastor. Maybe you can participate with another church or your local association. Most mission boards can help with planning as well.

One of the most common criticisms of short-term mission trips is the total expense for each trip. This is a legitimate issue that must be considered. The money spent on most short-term trips could fund a missionary family for several months and maybe a national pastor for several years. How should we think about these facts? The pointers below are not intended to solve all the issues, but perhaps they give some guidelines.

1. Remember the trip is not a luxury vacation. Be wise about expenses. Just because you can afford something, may not mean you should.
2. Before saying yes to a mission trip, ask hard questions about the potential long-term benefit of the trip. If your expenses

could support a family for months, does your trip have the potential to advance the cause by months or more? If not, say no to that trip and choose another one.

3. Keep in mind that God operates on a different economic scale. He owns the cattle on a thousand hills (Ps. 50:10), so he is not begging us for money. Remember, the money spent is not merely about travel logistics. It is an investment into helping you learn about and participate in God's mission. However, we are charged with being good stewards of what he gives us.
4. Meditate on the story in John 12. Mary poured a jar of expensive perfume on Jesus's feet, and one of the disciples complained it was a waste of money. Jesus shifted the conversation from expense to intent. Her actions demonstrated faith and worship. Could the same be said about your mission trip? I suspect this

> is the case for many trips; and, if so, the trip should not be considered a bad investment of money.

Volunteer with a local ministry. Look around your city. Where are other Christians engaged in missional activity? Are there ministries you can support with your time and personal activity. Perhaps your church has a partnership with a local ministry. Ask your pastor or mission team if there is any way you can join in. I have never known a growing ministry that had enough volunteer help!

As you join with others in ministry, your eyes and mind will be opened to the many needs that surround you. And it's okay if your first attempt is bumpy or doesn't seem to make as big an impact as you hoped. Keep praying. Keep showing up. Keep exploring. The Lord will be faithful to shape your heart toward his mission and calling. We often think we are too busy to do missions. But a few simple steps in the right direction will open many doors in our lives.

3. Ask God, "Why not me?" If you have made it this far, it is time for you to ask the life-changing question: "God, what is my role in obeying your Great Commission? Are you calling me to serve you as a missionary?" Seriously, do it now.

Go ahead. . . . I'll wait.

DISCUSS AND REFLECT

1. God's mission focuses on making disciples. What is your next step of obedience?

    - Who is someone specific you need to tell about Jesus? And someone else?
    - Who is a less mature Christian you need to help grow?
    - What area of your life does not reflect spiritual maturity?

2. How has this book helped you:

    - See the world differently?
    - Pray differently?
    - Understand God's will more fully?
    - Live with more conviction and confidence?

Conclusion

THIS BOOK HAS BEEN a journey through Jesus's final words in the book of Matthew. We have explored the internal and external implications of this passage. I hope this book will change the way you look at the world around you and also that it will change the way you see yourself in God's world.

The Bible tells us that God loved you and sent his Son Jesus to endure the punishment and shame of your sin. Jesus's death made it possible for you to enter into a right relationship with God and also to be adopted into his family. The Bible reminds us that each of us who has been saved has also been given the Spirit of adoption. This Holy Spirit dwells with us daily, moment by moment, as a partner in ministry. In other words, in Christ you are more than competent for the task ahead of you.

The challenge, as you close this book, is to keep your eyes and heart open. Consider these words by the famous missionary Hudson Taylor: "God isn't looking for people of great faith, but for individuals ready to follow him." This is most certainly why Jesus ends the Great Commission with the promise of his eternal presence: "I am with you always, even to the end of the age."

About the Author

D. Scott Hildreth is an associate professor of Missiology at Southeastern Baptist Theological Seminary. He teaches subjects related to missions, evangelism, cross-cultural ministry/living, and theology of missions.

Before coming to Southeastern Seminary, Scott and his family served with the International Mission Board (IMB) in Europe and Central Asia. Their work focused on Unreached Peoples and missionary development. It was his desire to encourage and equip more Christians to follow God's call to the mission field that brought them back to the U.S. and to the academy.

Scott has written several other books covering missions, Evangelism, ministry health, and a children's book on prayer.

Notes

Introduction

1. William Carey, "An Enquiry into the Obligation of Christians to Use Means for the Conversion of the Heathen," 1792, https://www.gutenberg.org/cache/epub/11449/pg11449-images.html.

2. Carey, "An Enquiry into the Obligation of Christians to Use Means for the Conversion of the Heathen."

3. Danny Akin, *10 Who Changed the World* (Nashville: B&H Publishing, 2012), 2.

4. David J. Bosch, *Transforming Mission: Paradigm Shifts in Theology of Mission* (Maryknoll, NY: Orbis Books, 2005), 390.

5. Bosch, *Transforming Mission*, 92.

6. Lesslie Newbigin, *The Open Secret: An Introduction to the Theology of Mission* (Grand Rapids: Eerdmans, 1995), Kindle loc. 253.

7. J. R. R. Tolkien, *The Lord of the Rings* (1954, 1955; reprint, Hammersmith, London: HarperCollins, 1991), 50.

Chapter 1

1. Donald Hagner, *Matthew 14–28*, vol. 33B, Word Biblical Commentary (Waco, TX: Word Book Publisher, 1995).

2. John Chrysostom, "Homily: 90.2, Gospel of Matthew," *Ancient Christian Commentary: Matthew 14–28*, vol 1B (Downers Grove, IL: InterVarsity Press).

3. C. S. Lewis, *Reflection on the Psalms*, in Selected Books (London: HarperCollins Religious, 1999), 694.

4. Lewis, *Reflection on the Psalms*, 695.

5. Lewis, *Reflection on the Psalms*, 695.

6. "The Best 18 Quotes from William Booth," *Caring Magazine* https://caringmagazine.org/the-best-18-quotes-from-william-booth/#:~:text=1.,the%20measure%20of%20his%20surrender.%E2%80%9D

7. John R. Stott, *The Message of Ephesians* (Downers Grove: InterVarsity Press, 1979), 163.

8. Robertson McQuilkin, "The Lost Apart from Christ," accessed March 26, 2024, https://www.cru.org/content/dam/cru/legacy/2012/03/Lost.pdf.

Chapter 2

1. Brother Andrew, *The God Smuggler*, Open Doors 60th Anniversary ed. (Bloomington MN: Chosen Books, 2015), 60.

2. C. S. Lewis, *Mere Christianity* in *C .S. Lewis: Selected Books* (London England: Harper Collins, 1999), 353.

3. Eric W. Heaton, *The Book of Daniel*, Torch Bible Commentary (London: SCM Press, 1956), 169.

4. Ben Witherington III, *Matthew*, Smyth & Helwys Commentary (Macon: Smith & Helwys, 2006), 532–33. See also Craig Blomberg, *Matthew*, New American Commentary (Nashville: Broadman, 1992), 431.

5. Leon Morris, *The Gospel according to Matthew*, The Pillar New Testament Commentary (Grand Rapids: Eerdmans, 1992).

6. Henry Blackaby, *Experiencing God: Knowing and Doing the Will of God* (Nashville: Lifeway Press, 2007), 134.

7. Morris, *The Gospel according to Matthew*.

8. John Stott in *Perspectives on the World Christian Movement*, 3rd ed. (Pasadena: William Carey Library, 1999), 21.

Chapter 3

1. Taken from People Groups, accessed February 20, 2024, https://peoplegroups.org.

2. Nicole Ward and Jeanne Batalove, "Refugees and Asylees in the United States," *Migration Policy Institute*, June 15, 2023, https://www.migrationpolicy.org/article/refugees-and-asylees-united-states.

3. Veera Korhonen, "Number of International Students in the U.S. 2022-23, by Country of Origin," *Statista*, July 5, 2024, https://www.statista.com/statistics/233880/international-students-in-the-us-by-country-of-origin.

4. Mohamad Moslimani and Jeffrey S. Passel, "What the Data Says about Immigrants in the U.S.," *Pew Research Center*, September 27, 2024, https://www.pewresearch.org/short-reads/2020/08/20/key-findings-about-u-s-immigrants.

5. According to the International Mission Board: "A people group is considered unreached (UPG) when there is no indigenous

community of believing Christians able to engage this people group with church planting. Technically speaking, the percentage of evangelical Christians in this people group is less than 2 percent." People Groups, accessed October 21, 2024, www.peoplegroups.org.

6. "What Is the 10/40 Window?," *Joshua Project*, accessed June 24, 2024, https://joshuaproject.net/resources/articles/10_40_window.

7. "World Watchlist 2024," *Open Doors*, June 24, 2024, https://www.opendoors.org/en-US/persecution/countries.

8. "What Is the 10/40 Window?," https://joshuaproject.net/resources/articles/10_40_window.

9. Charles Hadden Spurgeon, *The Soul Winner* (Grand Rapids: Eerdmans, 1989), 144.

Chapter 4

1. C. S. Lewis, *Mere Christianity* in *C .S. Lewis: Selected Books* (London England: Harper Collins, 1999), 323f.

2. Bridges and barriers is a missiological concept for identifying aspects of someone's worldview that either make it easier (bridges) or more difficult (barriers) for that person to understand and accept the claims of the gospel.

3. As Christians, we understand that the original world religion was the right worship of the one Creator God. The discussion in this section refers to the accepted framework of the origins of particular worship systems as practiced by people today.

4. Irvan Hexham, *Understanding World Religions: An Interdisciplinary Approach* (Grand Rapids: Zondervan, 2018), 183.

5. Timothy C. Tennent, *Theology in the Context of World Christianity: How the Global Church Is Influencing the Way We Think about and Discuss Theology* (Grand Rapids: Zondervan, 2007), 6.

6. Stanley J. Grenz, *A Primer on Postmodernism* (Grand Rapids: Eerdmans, 1996), 165.

7. Grenz, *A Primer on Postmodernism*.

8. Tennent, *Theology in the Context of World Christianity*, 61.

9. The Eightfold Path of Buddhism can get complicated to grasp in a short note but can be summarized as: (1) seeing things as they truly are and understanding the reality of and cause of suffering; (2) thinking accordingly; (3) speaking the truth; (4) acting and doing according to this teaching; (5) living in a manner that does not disrupt other life; (6) spending one's time doing good things and not becoming attached to anything; (7) being aware of one's thoughts at all times; (8) focusing one's mind and concentrating. Taken from: Derek Cooper, *Christianity and World Religions: An Introduction to the World's Major Faiths* (Phillipsburg, NJ: P&R Publishing, 2013), 39.

Chapter 5

1. Craig Blomberg, *Matthew*, New American Commentary (Nashville, TN: Broadman, 1992), 431.

2. David Bosch, *Transforming Mission: Paradigm Shifts in Theology of Mission* (Maryknoll: Orbis Books, 2005), 74.

3. Scot McKnight, "Kingdom Work, Social Justice," *Patheos*, October 21, 2011, https://www.patheos.com/blogs/jesuscreed/2011/10/21/kingdom-work-social-justice.

4. J. D. Payne, *Apostolic Imagination: Recovering a Biblical Vision for the Church's Mission Today* (Grand Rapids: Baker Academic, 2022), 28–29.

5. Wesley Duewel, *Touch the World through Prayer* (Grand Rapids, Zondervan, 1986), 21.

6. Nathan Finn, "Who will Hold the Ropes: A Plea for Great Commission Pastors and Churches," International Mission Board, June 28, 2017, https://www.imb.org/2017/06/28/hold-ropes-plea-pastors-churches.

7. Brother Andrew, "If I Perish," *Perspectives on the World Christian Movement: A Reader*, 4th ed. (Pasadena: William Carey Library, 2009), 193.

also available in the

SHORT GUIDE

series

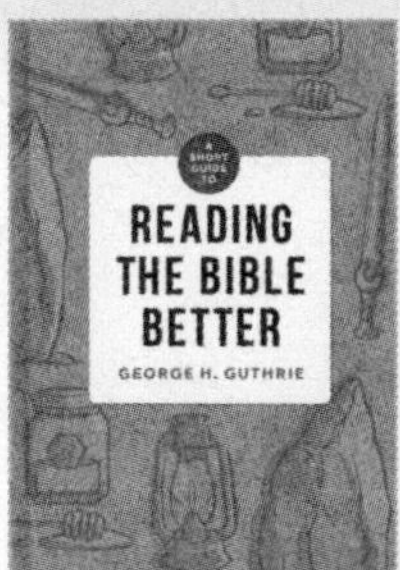